Saffron
Garlic
Olives
&

Saffron Garlic & Olives

Loukie Werle

FISHER
BOOKS™

Publishers: Howard W. Fisher, Helen V. Fisher
Managing Editor: Sarah Trotta
North American Editor: Jeanette Egan
Production Manager: Randy Schultz
Designed by: Denis Harman

First published in Australia in 1997 by
Simon & Schuster Australia
20 Barcoo Street, East Roseville NSW 2069
A Viacom Company
Sydney New York London Toronto Tokyo Singapore

Published by
Fisher Books, LLC
5225 W. Massingale Road
Tucson, Arizona 85743-8416
(520) 744-6110

Printed in U.S.A.
7 6 5 4 3 2 1

Library of Congress Cataloging-in-Publication Data
Werle, Loukie.
    Saffron garlic & olives / Loukie Werle.
        p. cm.
    ISBN 1-55561-184-2
    1. Cookery, Mediterranean. 2. Cookery (Saffron) 3. Cookery (Garlic) 4. Cookery (Olives)
    I. Title. II. Title: Saffron garlic and olives.

TX725.M35 W47 1999
641.59'1822 21—dc21   99-044960

Contents

Introduction

This book reflects how I feel about food. If that sounds selfish, I can only apologize and hope that the recipes provide the justification, because I think if there's no passion about food—and it has been the passion of many, many gifted people over the years that has inspired me—why bother at all?

Saffron, garlic and olives—exotic, earthy and ancient—seem to me to be all about passion, and are at the heart of the one cuisine that inextricably links the three, that of the Mediterranean.

As a child who was totally uninterested in food—for whom eating was a chore rather than a joy—the discovery of the flavors of the Mediterranean was a great turning point in my life. Fortunately, the revelation came when I was still young, on a vacation with my parents when I was in my early teens. Sitting on a sunny terrace above Lugano, Italy, I had my first taste of prosciutto with melon, followed by a huge bowl of garlicky mussels, served with good, crusty bread. It was bliss. I instantly recognized that my life had changed forever, and for the better.

Food should be delicious and fun first and foremost, and while I certainly didn't set out to write a book filled with "healthy" recipes, that's what it has become. With olive oil, garlic, onions and other fabulous vegetables, delectable pastas and risottos, inspiring beans and grains, plenty of fish and seafood, how could a book like this be other than good for the heart as well as the soul?

Saffron

The Exotic

Saffron is the henna-colored stigmas of the autumn-flowering crocus, *Crocus sativus*, and can only be gathered by hand during a harvest that lasts little more than two weeks. Each crocus bears only three stigmas. Knowing this, it should hardly be a surprise that saffron is the most expensive spice in the world. It is cultivated in far-flung parts of Spain, India, Turkey, Greece and the Abruzzi in southern Italy, where the saffron growers of the tiny village of Navelli believe they produce the finest in the world . . . though the farmers of La Mancha in Spain would disagree.

Because it's so exotic, saffron is often misunderstood. Take the color, a startling yellow that was used to dye the robes of the Israelites and the festive garments of Indians. The ancient Greeks considered it the color of royalty—though it was also adopted by the high-class prostitutes of the time—and no less a personage than Zeus slept on a bed of saffron. Many people still think of saffron mainly as a coloring agent, and it's true the tiniest amount will add a rich golden hue to an entire dish.

However, color is only part of it. The smell is wonderful; it always reminds me of honey, but others have said it's pungent, sweet or musky, and have even detected "a hint of burning tires." What's undeniable is that when you cook with saffron, it will fill your kitchen with a fragrance that's instantly recognizable and unlike any other.

As for the taste, it does wonders for fish and seafood, is the best of friends with tomatoes and fennel, and is indispensable when it comes to rice classics such as risotto Milanese and paella. It's also at home in sweet preparations such as saffron cakes and saffron sweet rolls, as well as the Pennsylvania Dutch Schwenkfelder cake.

The best way to buy saffron is in threads—the dried stigmas, which you'll find packed in small bags or containers in fine-food stores. There's also a powdered version, but be wary of that, especially if it seems to be a bargain, because there's an understandable temptation to adulterate saffron with cheaper coloring agents such as turmeric and safflower. The coloring will be strong, the taste won't.

Different people have different ways with saffron. I like to keep mine in an airtight container in the refrigerator (I once discovered to my dismay that weevils have a sophisticated bent). I prefer to soak the threads in a small amount of hot water before introducing the infusion into the other ingredients. I like the look of the whole threads in the finished dish, though some cooks choose to pulverize them. Others heat the threads first to make them brittle, and then pulverize them. The delicate stigmas can easily burn this way, making the saffron bitter. Adding too much saffron can also lead to a bitter result; only the smallest amount is needed, which means it's not so expensive after all and your precious supply will last for ages.

Food writer Waverley Root has said, "The use of saffron is only imaginable in a refined society, and a society that has time and money for the superfluous." To me, the whole idea of saffron is magical and its use is unimaginable only until you try it. Once you're under the spell of the crocus, you're bewitched forever.

Recipes

Saffron
Mayonnaise
(Rouille)

Rouille is a hot, spicy, thick sauce made from chiles, garlic, olive oil and breadcrumbs, potatoes or eggs. Here we are substituting a good-quality mayonnaise as the base. A debate rages about whether saffron should be present in rouille *("rust" in French) at all, as well as in that most famous of fish soups, bouillabaisse. Purists suggest not, claiming saffron belongs only in the soup itself, but most restaurants, even around Marseilles in Provence, add saffron to the* rouille *as well, possibly because it seems to be expected. The saffron mayonnaise is terrific when spread on slices of thick, toasted bread, floated in fish soups or stews, used in generous dollops to accompany cold fish or vegetable dishes (especially asparagus or artichokes), or as a dressing for fish or chicken salads.*

MAKES ABOUT 3/4 CUP (175ML)

1/4 teaspoon saffron threads

1 tablespoon hot water

1/2 teaspoon salt

2 dried red chiles, chopped

2 cloves garlic, peeled

3/4 cup (175ml) good-quality
  mayonnaise

Place the saffron in a small bowl and add the hot water. Let stand for at least 20 minutes or until needed. Combine the salt, chiles and garlic in a mortar and pound into a paste. Transfer to a food processor or blender; add mayonnaise and pulse until blended. Add the saffron and its soaking liquid and pulse until combined. Check seasoning, transfer to a bowl and serve immediately, or cover and refrigerate for up to 3 days.

Leek and Saffron Butter

This butter makes a deluxe sauce when placed on a freshly baked or grilled piece of fish, such as salmon, halibut, or sea bass. It's also great when tossed into hot pasta, rice or couscous.

MAKES 6 TO 8 SERVINGS

1-1/2 tablespoons dry white wine

1/2 teaspoon saffron threads

3 tablespoons unsalted butter, at room temperature

1 small leek, white part only, finely chopped

2 teaspoons lemon juice

Salt and black pepper

Hot pepper sauce

Heat the wine and pour it over the saffron threads in a small bowl. Let stand for at least 20 minutes or until needed.

Melt 2 teaspoons of the butter over low heat, add the leek and cook until soft, stirring frequently, about 5 minutes. Add the saffron and its soaking liquid and cook for 1 minute more. Remove from the heat and allow to cool. Stir in the lemon juice and season to taste with salt, pepper and hot pepper sauce.

Place the remaining butter in a food processor and process until creamy. Add the leek mixture and pulse until well combined. Scrape the butter into a small bowl and use immediately, or scrape onto a piece of plastic wrap, roll into a sausage shape and refrigerate or freeze until firm. Slice when needed.

Saffron Crêpes

There's something terribly attractive and "real" about cooking crêpes. Whenever I'm making crêpes, there never seems enough time to sit down and eat one myself, so it's a special pleasure to make them when no one else is around, and stack them neatly to be reheated later for starters or cut into smaller, bite-sized cocktail nibbles. Saffron crêpes are so attractive that you can serve them by themselves, with a squeeze of lemon juice. Tzatziki (see page 59) or Tapenade (see page 98) make great fillings, too.

MAKES 12 TO 16 SMALL CREPES

1/4 teaspoon saffron threads

1 tablespoon hot water

3/4 cup (175ml) milk

1/2 cup (120ml) water

3/4 cup (175ml) all-purpose flour

2 large eggs

1/2 teaspoon salt

2 tablespoons unsalted butter, melted

4 large fresh basil leaves, finely shredded

Unsalted butter, for cooking

Place the saffron in a small bowl and add the hot water. Let stand for at least 20 minutes or until needed.

Combine the milk, water, flour, eggs, salt and melted butter in a food processor or blender and process until smooth, stopping once to scrape down the sides. Pour into a pitcher or bowl, stir in saffron with its soaking liquid and basil, and let stand at least 1 hour.

To cook the crêpes, heat a crêpe pan over medium heat, add a little butter and swirl it around the pan. Pour about 2 tablespoons of batter into the pan and immediately rotate the pan, so the mixture thinly covers the bottom. Cook until little bubbles start to appear on the surface, flip over the crêpe. Cook until the other side is lightly browned. Serve immediately, or stack and cool. When wrapped in foil, they may be reheated in a 350F (180C) oven.

Saffron Gougère

Gougère, the famous French cheese pastry, is particularly popular in Burgundy, where it is eaten as an appetizer, either warm or at room temperature. However, it's made and enjoyed all over France. Traditionally, it is not made with saffron, but I think the addition elevates it to new heights. Also it freezes very well.

MAKES ABOUT 48

1/2 teaspoon saffron threads

1 tablespoon hot water

1/2 cup (120g) unsalted butter

1 cup (230ml) plus 2 tablespoons
water

Pinch of salt

1-3/4 (400ml) cups all-purpose flour

5 large eggs

8 oz. (240g) Gruyère cheese,
thinly sliced

Black pepper

1 egg, beaten

Preheat oven to 350F (180C). Lightly grease a baking sheet.

Place the saffron in a small bowl and add the hot water. Let stand for at least 20 minutes or until needed.

Combine the butter, water, saffron with its soaking liquid and the salt in a saucepan and bring to a boil. Remove from heat and add the flour, all at once. Mix well and return the pan to the heat. Stir over medium heat until the mixture forms a ball and comes away from the sides of the pan, about 2 minutes.

Remove from the heat and, using an electric mixer, beat in eggs, one at a time, until blended. This may be done in a food processor. Add cheese and pepper. Pipe or drop batter into 2-inch mounds about 1-1/2 inches (4cm) apart onto greased baking sheet. Brush with beaten egg.

Bake about 45 minutes or until firm and golden. Serve warm or at room temperature.

Fennel Tart with Sour Cream and Saffron

This elegant, yellow-hued tart is heaven on a plate. The pastry is extremely easy to handle, and provided you start with really cold, preferably frozen, butter, you can roll out the pastry immediately and fit it into the tart pan. On the other hand, if the butter isn't cold enough, it's safer to rest the pastry in the refrigerator for 30 to 60 minutes before rolling it out, to relax the gluten and prevent any shrinkage during baking.

MAKES 4 FIRST-COURSE SERVINGS

1/4 teaspoon saffron threads

3 tablespoons hot water

1 teaspoon cornstarch

2 teaspoons cold water

1 medium fennel bulb

1 tablespoon unsalted butter

4 tablespoons dry white wine

1/2 cup (120ml) regular or light
    sour cream

Salt and black pepper

3/4 cup (175ml) (3 oz.) grated
    Gruyère cheese

Pastry

1-1/2 cups (360ml) all-purpose flour

Pinch of salt

6 tablespoons unsalted butter, cold
    or frozen, cut into cubes

1 egg yolk

About 2 tablespoons iced water

Make the pastry first: Combine the flour, salt and butter in a food processor and pulse until the mixture resembles coarse breadcrumbs. Add the egg yolk. With the motor running, add just enough iced water through the feed tube to hold the mixture together. Remove to a floured surface and knead into a ball. Wrap in plastic wrap and refrigerate for 1 hour.

Preheat oven to 375F (190C). Lightly grease an 8-inch (20cm) tart pan with removable bottom.

On a lightly floured surface, flatten dough and

roll it out to a 10-inch (25cm) circle. Fit circle into the tart pan without stretching and trim off excess dough. Prick the bottom all over with a fork. Line with foil, following the contours of the pastry, and freeze for 30 minutes. Fill the foil-lined pastry shell with baking weights, dried beans or rice.

Bake for 10 minutes. Remove the foil and weights carefully and bake for 10 minutes more or until the pastry is pale golden and set. Decrease the oven temperature to 350F (180C).

Meanwhile make the filling. Place the saffron in a small bowl and add the hot water. Let stand for at least 20 minutes or until needed. Place the cornstarch in a small bowl and mix with the cold water until smooth. Set aside.

Cut the fennel bulbs (including the core) in half lengthwise, then cut into 1/4-inch-thick (0.6cm) slices. Melt the butter in a frying pan, add the fennel, and cook over medium-low heat until the fennel softens, stirring occasionally, 10 minutes. Add the wine

and sour cream, season to taste with salt and pepper, and simmer for 10 minutes more or until the sauce thickens slightly. Add the saffron and its soaking liquid and the cornstarch mixture. Cook, stirring, for 5 minutes more or until the fennel is coated with a rich, yellow sauce.

Spoon the fennel mixture into the tart shell and sprinkle with the cheese.

Bake about 30 minutes or until the tart is slightly puffed and golden. Serve warm or at room temperature.

Belgian Endive Wrapped in Prosciutto

This is one of my favorite starters for a winter dinner with friends. The whole thing can be put together ahead of time and, although very simple to prepare, the flavors are complex and satisfying, while the presentation is ravishing. In fact, it's so good you'll want this to be the whole meal, and I sometimes make double the quantity and serve it as supper with a simple salad.

MAKES 8 FIRST-COURSE OR 4 LIGHT MAIN-COURSE SERVINGS

1/4 teaspoon saffron threads

1 tablespoon hot water

8 heads Belgian endive

2 tablespoons extra-virgin olive oil

2 large onions, sliced

8 to 16 thin slices prosciutto (depending on size)

1/2 cup (120ml) dry white wine

Preheat oven to 375F (190C).

Place the saffron in a small bowl and add the hot water. Let stand for at least 20 minutes or until needed.

Add the Belgian endive to a pan of boiling, salted water, reduce heat and simmer until just starting to soften, 5 to 10 minutes, depending on size. Drain and place on one half of a clean dish towel, fold the towel over the endive and dry, gently pressing out as much moisture as possible.

Combine the oil and onions in a frying pan, add the saffron and soaking water; sauté over heat until the onions are orange-golden and tender, stirring frequently, about 10 minutes.

In a gratin dish, arrange the onions, covering the bottom completely. Wrap endive in 1 to 2 slices prosciutto, leaving the top and bottom exposed. Place on top of onions in one layer. Add the wine and cover with foil.

Bake 20 minutes or until the endive is tender. Remove foil and bake 10 minutes more to crisp the prosciutto slightly. Serve immediately on heated plates.

Garlic, Potato and Saffron Soup

This fabulous soup may be served either hot or cold. Either way, don't add the cream until just before serving, and if serving hot, make sure the soup does not boil again.

MAKES 4 FIRST-COURSE SERVINGS

2 heads garlic

2 teaspoons plus 2 tablespoons extra-virgin olive oil

1/4 teaspoon saffron threads

1 tablespoon hot water

1 large onion, chopped

2 medium baking potatoes, peeled and cubed

3-1/2 cups (820ml) water

Salt and black pepper

1 cup (230ml) light cream (optional)

Fresh lemon or lime juice

Preheat oven to 375F (190C).

Cut the top 1/3 inch (1cm) off the heads of garlic and drizzle each head with 1 teaspoon oil. Wrap securely in foil and bake 30 minutes, or until soft when pressed. Let cool.

Place the saffron in a small bowl and add the hot water. Let stand for at least 20 minutes or until needed.

Combine 2 tablespoons oil, onion and potatoes in a saucepan. Cook over medium heat until onion is soft, stirring frequently, 5 minutes. Add the water and bring to a boil. Cover and simmer until the potato is tender, 10 minutes.

Holding a roasted garlic bulb in one hand, squeeze the cloves from the head into the soup, one at a time. Purée the soup in a food processor or blender and return to the pan. Add the saffron and its soaking liquid. Season to taste with salt and pepper. Simmer for 5 minutes more, stirring occasionally.

If serving hot, add cream and a squeeze of lemon juice. If serving cold, pour into a heatproof bowl and refrigerate least 2 hours. Add the cream, if using, and the lemon juice. Season to taste before serving.

Pasta with Fava Beans, Saffron and Basil

Elegance personified, this delicate pasta is perfect as a first course or a light supper. Very young fava beans can be cooked after shelling; however, mature beans and their skins become tougher. It's better to peel them first. Place shelled beans in a pan of boiling water, return to a boil, drain immediately and run under cold water. Make a little cut with a sharp knife or fingernail and squeeze out the bean between thumb and forefinger.

MAKE 4 FIRST-COURSE OR LIGHT MAIN-COURSE SERVINGS

1/4 teaspoon saffron threads

1 tablespoon hot water

2 tablespoons extra-virgin olive oil

1 red onion, finely chopped

1-1/2 lb. (750g) fava beans, shelled

4 tablespoons finely shredded fresh basil

3 tablespoons dry white wine

Water

Salt and black pepper

12 oz. (360g) linguine or similar long pasta

Freshly grated pecorino or Parmesan cheese, to serve

Place the saffron in a small bowl and add the hot water. Let stand for at least 20 minutes or until needed.

Combine the oil and onion in a deep sauté pan and cook until the onion is soft, about 5 minutes. Add the beans and cook, stirring, for 1 minute. Add saffron and its soaking liquid, 3 tablespoons basil, white wine and enough water to barely cover. Season to taste with salt and pepper. Bring to a simmer; cover and cook over very low heat until the beans are tender, about 10 minutes. If there is too much liquid, uncover and briefly cook over medium heat.

Meanwhile, cook the pasta, drain and add to bean mixture. Toss together over medium heat for 2 minutes, sprinkle with remaining 1 tablespoon basil and serve immediately on heated plates. Serve cheese in a separate dish.

Mediterranean Fish Soup

This book wouldn't be complete without a fish soup. Here's something different. Chicken stock may surprise you, but I find fish stock can be too overpowering. Saffron Mayonnaise (see page 6) embellishes this soup handsomely.

MAKES 6 MAIN-COURSE SERVINGS

1/2 teaspoon saffron threads

2 tablespoons hot water

3 tablespoons extra-virgin olive oil

1 large red onion, chopped

1 carrot, peeled and thinly sliced

2 cloves garlic, finely chopped

1-1/2 lb. (725g) tomatoes, peeled and chopped

1/4 to 1/2 teaspoon hot chile flakes (optional)

3 cups (700ml) chicken stock

1-1/2 cups (360ml) dry white wine

1-1/2 cups water

2 (2-inch/6-cm) pieces orange zest

Salt and black pepper

3 lb. (1.4 kg) skinless white fish fillets, such as cod, sea bass or halibut, or a combination, cut into 1-1/2-inch (5cm) pieces

To serve

6 thick bread slices toasted

Saffron Mayonnaise (see page 6)

Place saffron in small bowl and add hot water. Let stand 20 minutes or until needed. Combine oil, onion and carrot in a large pot and sauté until soft, stirring frequently, about 5 minutes. Add garlic and cook, stirring, 1 minute. Add tomatoes, chile flakes, if using, saffron with soaking liquid, chicken stock, wine, water and orange zest. Season to taste with salt and pepper; simmer 20 minutes.

Bring mixture to a boil, add fish and boil 2 minutes, reduce heat and simmer 5 to 8 minutes. Discard orange zest and serve immediately, floating pieces of toasted bread spread with Saffron Mayonnaise on top. Or, purée the soup and serve in deep plates.

Moroccan Soup

(Harira)

During Ramadan, the Islamic month of fasting during the daylight hours, North African families sit down to this fragrant and robust soup at sundown. While visiting Morocco I was pleasantly surprised to find that harira is served at breakfast. It is accompanied by lemon wedges and fresh dates. The saffron flavor is pronounced in the heady mingling of spices, and the lemon and fresh cilantro give this soup a lightness belying its filling potential.

MAKES 8 FIRST-COURSE OR 4 MAIN-COURSE SERVINGS

3/4 cup (175ml) dried chickpeas

1/2 teaspoon saffron threads

2 tablespoons hot water

2 lb. (1 kg) ripe tomatoes, peeled and seeded, or 2 (14.5-oz./411g) cans tomatoes, with juice

1/2 teaspoon ground cinnamon

1/2 teaspoon ground turmeric

Salt and black pepper

2 tablespoons extra-virgin olive oil

1-1/2 lb. (750g) lean beef, cut into small cubes

2 large onions, chopped

1 stalk celery, thinly sliced

1 large clove garlic, finely chopped

8 cups (1.8 liters) cold water

3/4 cup (175ml) brown lentils

1 large egg, lightly beaten

3 oz. (90g) spaghetti, broken into short pieces

2 tablespoons all-purpose flour

6 tablespoons chopped fresh cilantro leaves

3 tablespoons chopped fresh parsley

Juice of 1 lemon

Lemon wedges and fresh dates, to serve

Place the chickpeas in a saucepan with 2 inches of water to cover. Bring to a boil; cook 1 minute and remove from heat. Cover and let stand for 1 hour at room temperature.

Place the saffron in a small bowl and add the hot water. Let stand for at least 15 minutes, or until needed. Combine the tomatoes, spices and saffron and its soaking liquid in a food processor or blender and process until smooth. Season with salt and black pepper and set aside.

Meanwhile, heat the oil in a Dutch oven over high heat. Add the beef, in batches, and sear on all sides until brown. (If the beef is crowded it will not brown.) Remove the beef with a slotted spoon and set aside. Add the onions and celery to the pan and cook over medium heat until onion is soft, about 5 minutes. Add garlic and cook for 1 minute.

Add puréed tomato mixture to the onion mixture. Return beef and any juices accumulated on the plate to the pan. Add 5 cups of water and the lentils. Drain the chickpeas, add them to the pan and bring to a boil. Simmer, covered, until the beef and chickpeas are tender, about 2 hours.

Stir the egg into the simmering soup, stirring vigorously to make strands. Add 2 cups (460ml) of the water, return to a simmer and stir in the spaghetti. Cook until the spaghetti is al dente, 8 to 10 minutes. Season to taste with salt and pepper. Blend flour with the remaining 1 cup (230ml) water. Bring soup to a boil and stir flour mixture into the soup. Simmer, stirring, 5 minutes. Stir in cilantro, parsley and lemon juice, and taste for seasoning. Serve in heated bowls with the lemon wedges and dates.

Tomato, Roasted Garlic and Saffron Soup

Mediterranean cuisine is unthinkable without the abundant use of ripe tomatoes, but it wasn't until 1570 that the Spaniards brought the tomato to Europe from Peru. This was in fact a yellow specimen, which the Italians called pomo d'oro or "golden apple," and the French named pomme d'amour, or "love apple," due to its reputed qualities as an aphrodisiac. In Italy, it wasn't until the 1700s that reference was made to the red tomato, and in France, as recently as the 1920s, the tomato would only be eaten when cooked.

MAKES 6 FIRST-COURSE SERVINGS

1 large head garlic

1 teaspoon plus 1 tablespoon extra-virgin olive oil

2 lb. (1kg) ripe tomatoes, peeled, seeded and chopped, or 2 (14.5 oz.) cans chopped tomatoes

1/4 teaspoon saffron threads

1 tablespoon hot water

1 onion, chopped

1 red bell pepper, chopped

4 large cloves garlic, finely chopped

1/2 cup (120ml) dry white wine

1/4 teaspoon hot chile flakes (optional)

1 bay leaf

4-3/4 cups (1.1 liters) chicken stock or water

Salt and black pepper

Lemon juice

Preheat oven to 375F (190C). Cut the top 1/3 inch (1cm) off the head of garlic and drizzle with the 1 teaspoon oil. Wrap securely in foil and bake for 30 minutes, or until soft when pressed. When cool enough to handle, hold the garlic head in one hand, and squeeze the cloves from the bulb into a food processor or blender. Add the tomatoes, pulse until smooth and set aside.

Meanwhile, place the saffron in a small bowl and add the hot water. Let stand for at least 20 minutes or until needed.

Combine remaining 1 tablespoon of oil in a large pan with onion; cook over medium heat until soft, about 5 minutes. Add bell pepper and chopped garlic, and cook until the bell pepper is tender, 8 to 10 minutes. Add wine and reduce to a glaze, about 2 minutes. Add reserved tomato and garlic purée, the saffron and its soaking liquid, chile flakes, if using, bay leaf and stock. Season to taste with salt and pepper. Simmer for 30 to 40 minutes. Taste for seasoning and add lemon juice, if desired, to bring out the flavor. Serve in heated bowls.

Pasta with Zucchini, Lemon and Saffron

I describe this pasta dish as gutsy, but delicate at the same time. The lemon and saffron flavors imbue the zucchini with character and vibrancy and, as always, the saffron color does wonders for pasta. The creamy effect is achieved by tossing the cooked pasta and vegetables with the cheese and the water in which the pasta was cooked.

MAKES 6 FIRST-COURSE OR 4 LIGHT
MAIN-COURSE SERVINGS

1/2 cup (120ml) dry white wine

1/4 teaspoon saffron threads

2 tablespoons extra-virgin olive oil

1 lb. (500g) zucchini, cut into
   2 x 1/2-inch (5 x 1-cm) strips

Salt and black pepper

1 red onion, halved and thinly sliced

4 cloves garlic, finely chopped

Juice of 2 lemons

1 lb. (500g) pasta such as buccatini,
   penne or rigatoni

4 oz./120g (1-1/3 cups) freshly
   grated Parmesan cheese

Heat wine in a small pan over medium heat, or in the microwave on MEDIUM for 20 seconds, then pour it over the saffron in a small bowl. Set aside at least 20 minutes or until needed.

Heat oil in a frying pan over medium-high heat until it just begins to smoke. Add the zucchini, in batches if necessary, and sauté until golden brown, shaking pan frequently, until the zucchini is crisp-tender, about 2 minutes. Transfer the zucchini to a plate and season to taste with salt and pepper. Cover loosely with foil to keep warm.

Add onion to the oil remaining in the pan and cook over medium heat until soft, stirring frequently, about 5 minutes. Add garlic and stir 1 minute more to release the aroma. Add lemon juice and the saffron and its soaking liquid, and stir until the liquid is reduced by half, 2 to 3 minutes. Keep warm. The onions will absorb the remaining liquid in the pan.

Meanwhile, cook the pasta in plenty of boiling, salted water until al dente. Drain and reserve about 1/2 cup (120ml) of the cooking liquid. Add pasta to the pan with the onion mixture, together with reserved zucchini and the cheese. Add a few tablespoons of the reserved water and toss over medium-high heat until the cheese and cooking water make a sauce and the zucchini is heated through, about 2 minutes. Serve immediately in heated bowls.

Risotto with Mushrooms, Radicchio and Saffron

If a chill is in the air, I like to serve this risotto at lunchtime. Although the saffron maintains a subtle presence, it works its magic in a felicitous marriage with the earthiness of the mushrooms and the faint bitterness of the radicchio. The radicchio may be replaced by arugula, spinach or Swiss chard.

MAKES 4 LIGHT MAIN-COURSE SERVINGS

1/4 teaspoon saffron threads

1 tablespoon plus 1 cup (240ml) hot water

1/3 oz./0.9g (about 10) dried porcini mushrooms

3 tablespoons extra-virgin olive oil

2 cloves garlic, finely chopped

10 fresh mushrooms

4-3/4 cups (1.1 liters) chicken stock

1 onion, finely chopped

1-3/4 cups/360g arborio rice

1/4 cup (60ml) dry white wine

Salt and black pepper

2 oz./60g (2/3 cup) freshly grated Parmesan cheese

1 head radicchio, shredded

Place the saffron in a small bowl and add the 1 tablespoon hot water. Let stand for at least 20 minutes or until needed. Place the porcini in another bowl and add the 1 cup (240ml) hot water. Let stand for 20 to 30 minutes, drain and reserve the soaking water. Trim and chop the fresh mushrooms and set aside. Drain the porcini soaking water through a sieve lined with a damp paper towel and set aside. Rinse the porcini.

Combine 1-1/2 tablespoons of the oil and the garlic in a frying pan over medium-low heat. Sauté until the garlic starts to soften, stirring frequently, about 3 minutes. Add the fresh mushrooms and the porcini, and cook over medium heat until the mushrooms are soft, tossing constantly, about 5 minutes. Keep warm over very low heat. Combine the stock and porcini soaking water in a saucepan over medium-low heat and bring to a steady simmer.

Combine the remaining oil in a pan with the onion and cook over medium heat until the onion is soft, stirring frequently, about 5 minutes. Stir in the rice and cook for 2 minutes, stirring constantly, until all the rice is coated with oil. Add the wine and cook, stirring constantly, until the wine is absorbed. Add the saffron and its soaking liquid, and a ladleful of the simmering stock. Stir until the liquid has been absorbed. Continue adding a ladleful of stock at a time until the rice is al dente, about 20 minutes, reserving about 3 tablespoons stock to stir in at the very end. Season to taste with salt halfway through the cooking process, and if the stock runs out before the rice is cooked, continue with simmering water.

When the rice is al dente, add the reserved stock, mushrooms, cheese and radicchio. Stir vigorously to combine, cover the saucepan and let stand off the heat for 3 minutes before serving. Serve in heated deep plates, seasoned with black pepper.

Pumpkin Risotto with Leek and Saffron

If you have a sweet tooth, this risotto is comfort food at its very best. The natural sweetness of pumpkin is subtly underscored by the use of leek instead of onion and, of course, saffron not only contributes a hint of honey, but also highlights the pumpkin color. I find this risotto delicious and satisfying, but because I have a savory rather than a sweet tooth, I would serve this as a starter, say instead of soup in the wintertime, rather than as a full meal.

MAKES 6 FIRST-COURSE OR 4 MAIN-COURSE SERVINGS

1/4 teaspoon saffron threads

1 tablespoon hot water

3 tablespoons extra-virgin olive oil

1 large or 2 small leeks (white and light green parts), finely chopped

2 small cloves garlic, finely chopped

1-3/4 cups/360g arborio rice

3/4 cup (175ml) dry white wine

1 lb. (500g) of pumpkin, peeled and seeds discarded, and flesh cut into 1/2-inch cubes

6 cups (1.4 liters) chicken stock or vegetable stock, simmering

Salt and black pepper

4 oz./20g (1-1/3 cups) freshly grated Parmesan cheese

3 tablespoons finely chopped fresh flat-leaf parsley

Place saffron in a small bowl and cover with the hot water. Let stand at least 20 minutes or until needed.

Combine oil and leek in a saucepan over medium-low heat and cook until soft, stirring frequently, about 8 minutes. Add garlic and cook about 1 minute. Stir in rice and cook 2 minutes, stirring constantly, until the rice is coated with oil. Add the wine and stir over medium heat until it is absorbed, 2 to 3 minutes.

Add the pumpkin and a ladleful of the simmering stock and stir until the stock has been absorbed. Continue adding stock and stirring until the rice is al dente, about 20 minutes. Do not add more stock until the previous amount has been absorbed. Add the saffron and its soaking liquid halfway through the cooking time, and season to taste with salt and pepper. Reserve a few spoonfuls of stock to stir in at the last moment.

When the rice is cooked, add cheese, parsley and reserved stock, and stir vigorously. Cover saucepan, remove from heat and let stand 3 minutes before serving. Serve in heated deep plates.

Risotto with Scallops, Saffron and Mascarpone

For lovers of scallops, this risotto makes a satisfying main course, although the delicate flavor suggests a starter. It may seem incongruous, but I use chicken stock rather than fish stock. The flavor of the scallops is dazzling, and powerful enough to carry the seafood theme without being aggressive. The scallops, saffron and mascarpone are first cooked separately into a quick stew, which also makes a splendid pasta sauce.

MAKES 6 FIRST-COURSE OR 4 MAIN-COURSE SERVINGS

Scallops, Saffron and Mascarpone

1/2 teaspoon saffron threads

2 tablespoons hot water

1/2 cup (120ml) dry white wine

1/2 onion, finely chopped

2 plum tomatoes, peeled, seeded and cut into small cubes

8 oz. (240g) bay scallops

4 oz./120g mascarpone

1/4 cup (60ml) chopped fresh flat-leaf parsley

Salt and black pepper

Risotto

2 tablespoons extra-virgin olive oil

1/2 onion, finely chopped

1-3/4 cups/360g arborio rice

1/2 cup (120ml) dry white wine

6 cups (1.4 liters) chicken stock, simmering

To make the scallops, saffron and mascarpone, place the saffron in a small bowl and add the hot water. Let stand for at least 20 minutes or until needed.

Combine the wine and onion in a frying pan and simmer over medium heat until the onion is soft, stirring frequently, about 5 minutes. Add tomatoes and the saffron and its soaking liquid, and cook over medium heat, stirring frequently, about 5 minutes, until liquid is reduced to about 1/4 cup. Add the scallops and cook until they turn opaque, about 2 minutes. Stir in the mascarpone and parsley and season to taste with salt and pepper. Simmer until mixture thickens slightly, about 3 minutes. Set aside.

To make the risotto, combine the oil and onion in a saucepan over medium heat and sauté until the onion is soft, stirring frequently, about 5 minutes. Stir in the rice and cook 2 minutes, stirring constantly, until the rice is coated with oil. Add the wine and stir until the rice absorbs it, about 2 minutes. Add a ladleful of the simmering stock and stir until it has been absorbed, about 3 minutes. Continue adding a ladleful of the stock after the previous one has been absorbed, until the rice is al dente, about 20 to 25 minutes. Season lightly with salt and pepper about halfway through the cooking time. If the stock runs out, continue with simmering water.

When the rice is cooked, stir in scallop mixture, just to warm through. Cover the saucepan, remove from the heat, and let stand for 3 minutes. Serve in heated deep plates.

Saffron Rice Salad with Shrimp, Olives and Radicchio

This is one of my favorite summer salads and can be made in advance, although when refrigerating it longer than 30 minutes, I don't add the radicchio until just before serving. Make sure you add the crisp, white bottom parts of the radicchio leaves as well as the softer red areas. The white parts contribute a delicious, savory bitterness and crunch to the salad. Sometimes, instead of shrimp, I make this with grilled chicken with the skin on.

MAKES 4 MAIN-COURSE SERVINGS

Shrimp

1 lb. (500g) large shrimp, peeled and deveined, tails intact

2 large cloves garlic, finely chopped

1/2 teaspoon hot chile flakes

1 tablespoon lemon juice

2 tablespoons extra-virgin olive oil

Salt and black pepper

1/2 teaspoon saffron threads

1-1/4 cups/300g arborio rice

2 tablespoons lemon juice

4 tablespoons (60ml) extra-virgin olive oil

3 oz. (120g) ripe olives, preferably kalamata, pitted and halved

1 red onion, finely diced

1 radicchio, rinsed and torn into bite-sized pieces, including the core

3 tablespoons chopped fresh flat-leaf parsley

Prepare the shrimp first: Combine shrimp in a bowl with garlic, chile flakes, lemon juice and oil, and season with salt and pepper. Toss gently, cover and refrigerate 30 minutes. Cook on a hot grill, under a broiler or in a cast-iron skillet until opaque, about 4 minutes. Set aside.

Meanwhile, place the saffron in a small bowl and cover with the hot water. Let stand at least 20 minutes or until needed.

Cook the rice in 2-1/4 cups (520ml) lightly salted, boiling water until tender and water is absorbed, about 20 minutes. Transfer to a large bowl.

Combine the saffron and its soaking liquid in a small bowl with the lemon juice. Drizzle in the oil, whisking constantly. Pour saffron mixture over the rice and toss. Add the shrimp, olives, onion, radicchio and parsley, and toss well. Taste for seasoning and serve immediately. If making ahead, omit the radicchio, cover and refrigerate until just before serving. Add the radicchio and allow to return to room temperature before serving.

Spanish Lima Bean Stew with Ham, Chorizo and Saffron

Chorizo, popular in Spain and Mexico, has taken the rest of the western world by storm. This coarse-textured, spicy sausage is usually made with pork and a good amount of garlic. Fresh sausages may be cooked in soups and stews. To rid the fresh sausages of excess fat, place them in boiling water and simmer for 5 minutes before adding them to the other ingredients.

While for most beans the quick-soak method works perfectly, I like to make an exception for lima beans. These large beans tend to burst out of their thin skin with the quick-soak, so take the slow route and you'll end up with creamy-smooth, billowy puffs.

MAKES 4 MAIN-COURSE SERVINGS

1/4 teaspoon saffron strands

1 tablespoon hot water

2 tablespoons extra-virgin olive oil

1 large red onion, coarsely chopped

2 stalks celery, chopped, including leaves

2 cloves garlic, finely chopped

1 lb. (500g) dried lima beans, soaked overnight in water to cover

8 oz. (240g) cooked ham, cut into bite-sized pieces

4 fresh chorizo sausages

About 1/4 cup (60ml) fresh flat-leaf parsley, roughly chopped

Place the saffron in a small bowl and cover with the hot water. Let stand at least 20 minutes or until needed.

Preheat oven to 375F (190C).

Combine the oil, onion and celery in Dutch oven or flameproof casserole dish over medium-low heat and cook until soft, stirring frequently, 10 to 15 minutes.

Add the garlic and cook until aromatic, 1 minute.

Drain the beans, rinse well and add to the pan, with the ham, chorizo and the saffron and its soaking liquid. Add enough water to barely cover, stir well and bring slowly to a boil. Cover and place in the oven. Bake 1-1/2 hours or until the beans are tender. If there is too much liquid, remove the sausages and cook, uncovered, over medium-high heat until the liquid has reduced. Return the sausages, stir in the parsley, and serve in heated bowls.

Swordfish and Potato Stew with Saffron and Cilantro

The inclusion of cumin and lemon juice, as well as the aromatic saffron and cilantro, places this fabulous dish firmly in the cuisine of North Africa, or more specifically, Tunisia. Though uncomplicated to prepare, it gives its more famous Provençal cousin, bouillabaisse, a challenging run for its money. Strictly speaking it is a soup; I like to serve this as a main dish with good crusty bread.

In a pinch, you may use purchased ground cumin, but taking the trouble to roast and grind the spices yourself pays off handsomely in flavor dividends. Take my advice and throw out any old ground spices lurking in your pantry, buy only whole seeds at a shop with a good turnover, and replace them regularly.

MAKES 4 MAIN-COURSE SERVINGS

1/4 teaspoon saffron threads

1 tablespoon hot water

1/2 teaspoon cumin seeds

2 tablespoons extra-virgin olive oil

3 large cloves garlic, finely chopped

2 large tomatoes, peeled, each cut into 8 wedges

1 teaspoon mild paprika

1/4 teaspoon hot chile flakes

7 tablespoons chopped fresh cilantro leaves

2 tablespoons chopped fresh flat-leaf parsley

4-1/4 cups (1.1 liters) water

Juice of 1 lemon

Salt and black pepper

1 lb. (500g) waxy potatoes, peeled and cut into 1/2-inch (1cm) slices

1-1/2 lb. (750g) swordfish steaks, cut into bite-sized pieces

Crusty bread, to serve

Place the saffron in a small bowl and cover with the hot water. Let stand at least 20 minutes or until needed.

Place the cumin seeds in a dry small frying pan and roast over medium heat, shaking the pan from time to time, until the seeds are aromatic and small wisps of smoke start to escape, about 3 minutes. Be careful not to burn the seeds. Pulverize in a mortar and set aside.

Combine the oil and garlic in a Dutch oven and cook over medium-low heat, stirring frequently, until the garlic softens, about 3 minutes. Add the tomatoes, the saffron and its soaking liquid, ground cumin, paprika, chile flakes, 6 tablespoons of the cilantro and the parsley, and cook over medium heat 5 minutes, stirring frequently.

Add the water, lemon juice, salt and pepper to taste, and the potatoes. Bring to a boil, reduce the heat to low and cover. Simmer until the potatoes are tender, about 20 minutes.

Add the fish and simmer until opaque and cooked through, about 5 minutes. Taste for seasoning, sprinkle with the remaining cilantro and serve immediately in heated deep plates, with plenty of crusty bread.

Rice with Cheese, Saffron and Herbs

There are those who will always choose a risotto when spotted on a restaurant menu, because they think it's too much work to make at home. Personally, I think this is crazy for two reasons: Stirring a risotto is one of the most pleasant tasks in the kitchen, provided you have the right equipment and ingredients, a good glass of wine to drink and fabulous music to listen to. Second, risotto is one of those dishes that's so much better when made at home. Most restaurants use an interrupted method, and the result doesn't compare with a properly stirred risotto.

This stunning rice dish—but never call it a risotto—is for those times when you're too busy with other important things, such as helping the kids with their homework or catching up on the day's events with your dinner guests.

MAKES 4 MAIN-COURSE SERVINGS

1/4 teaspoon saffron threads

1 tablespoon hot water

1 cup (230ml) arborio or other short-grain rice

8 oz. (240g) bocconcini (marinated fresh small mozzarella balls), preferably buffalo mozzarella, drained and chopped

4 oz./20g (1-1/3 cups) freshly grated Parmesan cheese

About 1/2 cup (120ml) fresh basil leaves, torn

About 1/4 cup (60ml) fresh flat-leaf parsley, roughly chopped

Salt and black pepper

Place the saffron in a small bowl and cover with the hot water. Let stand for at least 20 minutes or until needed.

Meanwhile, cook the rice in 1-3/4 cups (425ml) lightly salted, boiling water until tender and the water is absorbed, about 20 minutes.

Immediately spoon half the rice into a heated deep bowl. Sprinkle with the mozzarella, Parmesan, herbs and the saffron and its soaking liquid. Season lightly with salt and pepper, then spoon the remaining hot rice on top. Toss thoroughly with two large forks and serve immediately in heated deep plates.

Sicilian Pasta with Cauliflower and Saffron

The Arab influence can be keenly felt in the exotic combination of flavors in this otherwise simple pasta dish. The Saracens ruled over the island of Sicily for two centuries and in many ways—architectural, religious, cultural and gastronomical—left their unmistakable imprint.

MAKES 4 LIGHT MAIN-COURSE SERVINGS

1/4 teaspoon saffron threads

3 tablespoons hot water

3 tablespoons dried currants

4 tablespoons blanched almonds

Salt and black pepper

1 cauliflower, divided into bite-sized florets

12 oz. (360g) short pasta, such as penne or rigatoni

2 tablespoons extra-virgin olive oil

1 large onion, chopped

4 cloves garlic, finely chopped

Preheat oven to 350F (180C). Place the saffron in a small bowl and add the hot water. Let stand for at least 20 minutes or until needed.

Place currants in another bowl and cover with hot water. Let stand 20 minutes and then drain.

Place almonds on a baking sheet. Roast 10 to 15 minutes, or until golden. Cool and chop coarsely.

Fill a large pot with water, bring to a boil and add salt. Add cauliflower and cook until crisp-tender, 4 to 5 minutes. Remove cauliflower, reserving the water for the pasta. Cook pasta in the water.

Meanwhile, combine the oil and onion in a large, deep sauté pan and cook until soft, stirring frequently, about 5 minutes. Add garlic and cook 1 minute more. Add saffron and its soaking liquid, currants, cauliflower and almonds. Toss well and keep sauce warm. Drain pasta and add to cauliflower mixture. Toss over medium heat for 2 minutes and serve immediately.

Tomato and Fish Stew with Saffron

A delectable but quick-and-easy fish stew, guaranteed to become a regular in your repertoire, as it has in mine. It's just the thing for unexpected guests, or for a family meal. Any firm-fleshed, white fish fillets will do.

MAKE 4 MAIN-COURSE SERVINGS

1/2 teaspoon saffron threads

2 tablespoons hot water

2 tablespoon extra-virgin olive oil

1-1/2 lb. (750g) white fish fillets, such as halibut, cod or sea bass, cut into 1/2-inch (1cm) cubes

1 leek (white part), thinly sliced

4 cloves garlic, chopped

1 cup (230ml) dry white wine

4 tomatoes, peeled and chopped

3 tablespoons chopped fresh flat-leaf parsley

Crusty bread, to serve

Place the saffron in a small bowl and cover with the hot water. Let stand at least 20 minutes or until needed.

Heat a large nonstick frying pan over medium heat. Add 1 tablespoon of oil and the fish. Sauté until all sides are seared, about 2 minutes. Remove from the pan and set aside.

Add remaining 1 tablespoon of oil and the leek to the pan. Sauté over medium heat until the leek is soft, about 4 minutes.

Add garlic; cook 2 minutes, stirring constantly.

Stir in the wine and the saffron with its soaking liquid, cook 2 minutes more, and then add the tomatoes and parsley. Cook uncovered until the sauce thickens, about 10 minutes. Return fish to the pan and simmer over low heat until cooked through, about 5 minutes. Serve with plenty of crusty bread to mop up the juices.

Butterflied Garlic Shrimp with Saffron

Prepared in just a few minutes, this dish has definite drama. Perfect for a summer lunch or light dinner, I like to serve these shrimp on a bed of cannellini beans, either warm or, when the weather's really hot, at room temperature. Rice makes a reasonable substitute. Be sure not to boil away all the cooking juices, because these bathe whatever's underneath the shrimp—such as beans, rice or couscous—with their vibrant color.

MAKES 4 LIGHT MAIN-COURSE SERVINGS

2 tablespoons lemon juice

1/2 teaspoon saffron threads

1-1/2 lb. (750g) large shrimp, peeled and deveined, tails intact

2 tablespoons extra-virgin olive oil

4 cloves garlic, finely chopped

1/4 teaspoon hot chile flakes

1 tablespoon chopped fresh oregano

2 tablespoons dry white wine

Salt and black pepper

1 tablespoon finely chopped fresh flat-leaf parsley

Warm the lemon juice in the microwave on MEDIUM for 20 seconds and pour over the saffron in a small bowl. Set aside for at least 20 minutes or until needed.

To butterfly the shrimp, deepen the incision where you have taken out the vein with a sharp knife, being careful not to cut completely through. Flatten the shrimp with the flat blade of the knife and set aside.

Combine the oil and garlic in a large frying pan over medium-low heat and cook, stirring constantly, until the garlic softens, about 3 minutes. Increase the heat to high; add chile flakes and oregano and cook, stirring, 1 minute. Add shrimp and cook 1 minute on each side, pressing down on shrimp with a spatula to keep them from curling. Add the saffron and lemon mixture and the wine, and cook the shrimp, turning, until yellow on both sides, 30 to 60 seconds. Season to taste with salt and pepper and serve immediately, sprinkled with parsley.

Pan-fried Fish Fillets with Tomato, Saffron and Garlic Sauce

You need only a few short minutes to cook this irresistible dish for your guests, especially if all the ingredients are chopped and otherwise prepared (the French call this mise en place). *I like to serve this with golden, crisp, oven-roasted potato chunks strewn with thyme sprigs, but thick slices of crusty bread aren't amiss. To stick with the North African flavor theme, couscous makes a natural companion. Serve a crisp green salad to follow.*

MAKES 4 MAIN-COURSE SERVINGS

1/4 teaspoon saffron threads

1 to 2 tablespoons hot water

1/2 teaspoon cumin seeds

1/4 teaspoon coriander seeds

2 tablespoons extra-virgin olive oil

4 cloves garlic, finely chopped

2 tablespoons lemon juice

2 tomatoes, peeled and cut into small cubes

Salt and black pepper

4 firm, white fish fillets, such red snapper or sea bass

2 tablespoons finely chopped fresh flat-leaf parsley

Place saffron in a small bowl; cover with hot water. Let stand 20 minutes or until needed.

Combine the cumin and coriander seeds in a small dry frying pan and roast over medium heat, shaking the pan occasionally. Take care not to burn the seeds. Cool for a few minutes, then pulverize in a mortar and set aside.

Combine oil and garlic in a frying pan large enough to hold the fish fillets in one layer. Cook, stirring occasionally, over medium-low heat until the garlic starts to soften, but without coloring, about 2 minutes. Add lemon juice, the saffron and its soaking liquid, ground spices and tomatoes; season to taste with salt and pepper. Cook over medium heat 5 minutes, stirring frequently.

Place fish, without overlapping, on top of the sauce. Spoon some sauce over the fish, cover the pan with a lid and cook over low heat until fish is cooked through, 10 to 15 minutes. Serve immediately, sprinkled with parsley.

Fish Fillets Poached in Wine with Saffron and Parsley

The delicate action of poaching preserves the intrinsic flavors and texture of the fish, while the liquid becomes a magnificently fragrant, yellow sauce. This is delicious served with roasted potatoes or couscous.

MAKES 4 MAIN-COURSE SERVINGS

1/2 teaspoon saffron threads

2 tablespoons hot water

1 cup (230ml) dry white wine

1 cup (230ml) water

2 cloves garlic, finely chopped

3 tablespoons extra-virgin olive oil

4 thick fish fillets, such as haddock, swordfish or halibut

Salt and black pepper

1 large lemon, peeled and cut into wafer-thin slices

2 tablespoons finely chopped fresh flat-leaf parsley

Place the saffron in a small bowl and cover with the hot water. Let stand at least 20 minutes or until needed.

In a deep frying pan that will hold the fish in one layer, combine the wine, water, garlic, oil and the saffron and its soaking liquid, and bring to a boil. Boil 1 minute.

Season the fish with salt and pepper. Reduce the heat so the liquid barely shivers on the surface, without bubbles breaking.

If necessary, use a heat diffuser. Lower the fish gently into the liquid, distribute the lemon slices on top and cover the pan with a lid or foil. Cook over low heat until the fish is opaque at its thickest point, and the flesh flakes easily, 10 to 15 minutes, depending on the thickness of the fish. Serve immediately on heated plates. Sprinkle with parsley and a little of the sauce.

Tuna and Fennel Stew with Saffron

Although this recipe, minus the saffron, previously appeared in my book Trattoria Table, I don't hesitate to include it here. As so often happens, when you cook a particular recipe frequently, it evolves with time. Good as it was before, the flavor of this light but satisfying dish improves dramatically with the addition of saffron. Instructions are included to thicken the sauce, if desired. Personally, I prefer the lightness of a thinner consistency.

MAKES 4 MAIN-COURSE SERVINGS

1/4 teaspoon saffron threads

1 tablespoon hot water

1 large fennel bulb, thinly sliced, and the feathery leaves reserved

3 tablespoons extra-virgin olive oil

1 large onion, chopped

2 cloves garlic, finely chopped

1 lb. (500g) tomatoes, peeled, seeded and chopped, or 1 (14.5-oz./411g) can tomatoes, chopped, with juice

2 bay leaves

3 tablespoons chopped fresh flat-leaf parsley

1 generous strip lemon zest

2 tablespoons lemon juice

2 lb. (1kg) fresh tuna, cut into bite-sized cubes

1/2 cup (120ml) dry white wine

1 to 2 cups (230 to 460ml) fish stock or light chicken stock

Salt and black pepper

Crusty bread, to serve

Place the saffron in a small bowl and cover with the hot water. Let stand at least 20 minutes or until needed.

Combine fennel and oil in a Dutch oven over medium heat and cook, stirring frequently, until fennel starts to soften, about 5 minutes. Add onion and cook, stirring, until it softens, about 5 minutes. Add garlic and cook 1 minute. Add tomatoes and cook 5 minutes, stirring frequently. Add bay leaves, parsley, lemon zest and juice, tuna, wine and the saffron and its soaking water.

Add enough stock to cover the fish and simmer until the fish is cooked through, about 10 minutes. Discard the bay leaves and lemon zest.

If you wish to thicken the sauce, remove fish and vegetables to a bowl and reduce the liquid in the pan until slightly thickened. Return the tuna and vegetables, and season to taste with salt and pepper.

Sprinkle with fennel leaves, and serve with crusty bread to mop up the juices.

Potato, Mussel and Rice Gratin with Saffron

Every Italian homemaker seems to have her own version of this recipe, jealously guarded from generation to generation. The moment the mussels are removed from the heat, it's important to move quickly, because the mussel liquid is used to soak the saffron; once the liquid is lukewarm, you just won't get the best out of your precious saffron.

MAKES 4 MAIN-COURSE SERVINGS

2 lb. (1 kg) mussels in shells

Salt and black pepper

1/4 teaspoon saffron threads

2 cloves garlic, finely chopped

3 tablespoons chopped fresh
 flat-leaf parsley

1-1/2 lb. (750g) waxy potatoes
 (about 4 medium), boiled for
 6 minutes, then thinly sliced

1 large onion, thinly sliced

1 cup/210g arborio rice

4 plum tomatoes, thinly sliced

2 cups (460ml) fresh breadcrumbs

2 tablespoons extra-virgin olive oil

Place the mussels in a clean sink, cover with cold water and add a few tablespoons of salt. Discard any mussels that won't close when tapped. Add a few tablespoons of salt and soak 1 hour. Remove beards and scrub the shells, if necessary.

Meanwhile, place saffron in a bowl and set aside. Preheat oven to 375F (190C). Lightly oil a gratin dish.

Transfer the mussels to a large pan with the water clinging to them. Place over high heat and, shaking the pan frequently, cook until the mussels open, 4 to 7 minutes. Discard any mussels that have not opened. With tongs, remove cooked mussels to a bowl. Strain the mussel liquid, through a strainer lined with damp paper towels, into the bowl containing the saffron threads. Let stand at least 20 minutes or until needed.

Remove mussels from the shells and, while still warm, combine with half of the garlic and parsley.

Layer half of the potatoes in the gratin dish, season

with salt and pepper, then add half the onion. Sprinkle evenly with the rice and cover with the mussels. Cover with the tomatoes, season with salt and pepper and top with the remaining onion, garlic and parsley. Cover with the remaining potatoes and season with salt and pepper. Sprinkle with the breadcrumbs and drizzle with the oil. Pour the reserved mussel and saffron liquid over the top, and add enough hot water to barely cover the top potato layer. Cover with foil.

Bake 45 minutes or until the potatoes are tender.

Remove the foil and bake 10 to 15 minutes more or until the top is golden and crunchy. Serve immediately.

Meatballs in Saffron and Garlic Tomato Sauce

The saffron in this fresh tomato sauce elevates these humble meatballs into a meal to be shared on festive occasions, rather than something you only make for the children (or for yourself when you're scraping the bottom of the piggy bank). The uncooked rice in the meatball mixture requires long, slow cooking to ensure tenderness.

Meatballs

1 teaspoon cumin seeds

1/3 cup (80ml) arborio rice

Boiling water, to cover

1 lb. (500g) lean ground beef

1 small red onion, finely chopped

2 large cloves garlic, finely chopped

1 teaspoon chopped fresh oregano leaves

2 tablespoons chopped fresh flat-leaf parsley

Salt and black pepper

3 tablespoons extra-virgin olive oil

Saffron and Garlic Tomato Sauce

1/2 teaspoon saffron threads

2 tablespoons hot water

1 small red onion, finely chopped

4 large cloves garlic, finely chopped

2 lb. (1kg) tomatoes, peeled, seeded and chopped

Salt and black pepper

3 tablespoons chopped fresh flat-leaf parsley

1 tablespoon finely chopped fresh basil

To make the meatballs, place the cumin seeds in a small, dry frying pan and roast over medium heat until aromatic and starting to color, about 3 minutes. Allow to cool, pulverize in a mortar, and set aside.

Place the rice in a small bowl and pour enough boiling water over to cover. Let stand 5 minutes, then drain. Combine ground cumin and rice in a large bowl with the beef, onion, garlic and herbs. Season with salt and pepper. Fry a small amount and taste to check seasoning. With wet hands, shape the mixture into 8 equal balls.

Heat the oil in a large, preferably cast-iron, Dutch oven over medium-high heat. Add meatballs and fry until browned all over. Set meatballs aside on a plate. Set pan aside.

To make the tomato sauce, place the saffron in a small bowl and cover with the hot water. Set aside 20 minutes or until needed.

Meanwhile, add the onion to the oil remaining in the Dutch oven and cook over medium heat, stirring frequently, until soft, about 5 minutes. Add the garlic and cook until aromatic, 1 minute. Add the tomatoes and the saffron with its soaking liquid and season with salt and pepper. Simmer until the sauce has slightly thickened, about 10 minutes. Add the

meatballs with any juices accumulated on the plate, and enough water to barely cover. Bring to a simmer, cover and cook over low heat 30 minutes, checking occasionally that the liquid is simmering gently and the meatballs are covered with the sauce. Serve immediately, sprinkled with the parsley and basil.

Chicken and Fennel Stew with Saffron

A variation on the bouillabaisse theme, this time with chicken in the starring role, and using a simple cooking method. All the fragrant ingredients are assembled in the Dutch oven the day before cooking, so the flavors mingle and develop. The next day you simply put it on the stove to cook.

I like to use boneless chicken thighs when making stews or curries. They're inexpensive, there's hardly any waste and they're very forgiving when it comes to cooking them just right.

MAKES 6 MAIN-COURSE SERVINGS

1/4 teaspoon saffron threads

2 lb. (1kg) boneless chicken thighs

2 large red onions, cut into 8 wedges each

2 fennel bulbs, 1-1/2 lb. (750g) each, cut into 1/2-inch (1cm) slices through the bottoms, feathery leaves reserved

4 tomatoes, peeled, seeded, chopped

4 cloves garlic, finely chopped

1/4 teaspoon hot chile flakes (optional)

3/4 cup (175ml) dry white wine

2 tablespoons extra-virgin olive oil

1/4 cup (60ml) fresh thyme sprigs

1 lb. (500g) waxy potatoes

1 to 2 cups (230-460ml) chicken stock

Salt and black pepper

3 tablespoons chopped fresh flat-leaf parsley

Crusty bread, to serve

Place the saffron in a small bowl and add the hot water. Set aside at least 20 minutes or until needed.

Meanwhile, combine chicken, onions, fennel, tomatoes, garlic, chile flakes, if using, wine, oil and thyme in a Dutch oven. Add saffron and its soaking liquid, toss to coat all ingredients. Cover and refrigerate overnight.

Remove Dutch oven from refrigerator and stand at room temperature 1 hour, then place over low heat and bring to a simmer. Simmer gently 30 minutes. Cut potatoes into 3/4-inch (2cm) pieces and add to chicken mixture. Add enough stock to barely cover, and season with salt and pepper. Bring to a simmer again, cover and simmer gently until the potatoes are tender, 30 minutes. Taste for seasoning and sprinkle with reserved fennel leaves and parsley. Serve in heated deep bowls with crusty bread.

Grilled Chicken in Cilantro and Saffron Marinade

This marinade is typical of North Africa, with fragrant fennel, fresh cilantro, ginger and saffron. Any kind of chicken works well: Try thighs or breasts with bone in and skin on, or skinned and boned. A whole chicken may be marinated and barbecued or oven-roasted.

MAKES 4 MAIN-COURSE SERVINGS

1/2 teaspoon saffron threads

1 tablespoon fennel seeds

2-inch (5-cm) piece fresh ginger, thickly sliced

4 cloves garlic, roughly chopped

2 hot red chiles, roughly chopped

2 teaspoons mild paprika

1/4 cup (60ml) lemon juice

1 bunch fresh cilantro leaves, chopped

8 green onions, roughly chopped

1 cup (230ml) extra-virgin olive oil

Salt and black pepper

1 (2-1/2 to 3-lb. /1-1.5 kg) chicken, cut into pieces, or 4 chicken breasts or 4 chicken legs

Lemon wedges, to serve

Place the saffron in a small bowl and add the hot water. Let stand at least 20 minutes or until needed.

Place fennel seeds in a dry small frying pan and roast over medium heat until fragrant and starting to color, shaking the pan frequently, about 3 minutes. Transfer to a mortar and pulverize. Set aside.

Combine ginger, garlic and chiles in a food processor or blender and pulse until chopped. Add saffron and its soaking liquid, ground fennel seeds, paprika and lemon juice, and blend into a paste. Add cilantro and green onions, and process until finely chopped. With the machine running, add the oil in a steady stream through the feed tube. Season to taste with salt and pepper.

Place the chicken in a bowl, pour over the marinade and turn to coat. Cover bowl with plastic wrap and refrigerate overnight.

About 30 minutes before cooking, remove chicken from refrigerator and bring to room temperature. Preheat grill. Drain chicken; reserve marinade. Grill chicken, basting frequently with the marinade, until juices run clear when the chicken is pierced in the thickest part, about 30 minutes, depending on size. Small pieces may need to removed sooner. Serve hot with lemon wedges.

Roast Lemon Chicken with Saffron Sauce

This is one of my favorite ways to roast a chicken; there's plenty of flavor in the chicken from the lemon, garlic and oregano, with the added bonus of a rich, yellow sauce, which is made like a mayonnaise, but uses cooked egg yolks. The whites are chopped and added to the sauce for textural interest.

MAKES 4 MAIN-COURSE SERVINGS

1 tablespoon extra-virgin olive oil

Grated zest of 1/2 lemon

Juice of 1 lemon (reserve the squeezed lemon halves)

2 cloves garlic, finely chopped

1 tablespoon chopped fresh oregano leaves

Salt and black pepper

1 (3-lb./1.5kg) whole chicken

Saffron Sauce

1/4 teaspoon saffron threads

2 tablespoons hot water

2 large eggs, hard-cooked, yolks and whites separated

1 clove garlic, roughly chopped

1 tablespoon lemon juice

3 tablespoons extra-virgin olive oil

Salt and black pepper

Combine the oil, lemon zest and juice, garlic and oregano in a large bowl. Whisk together and season to taste with salt and pepper. Add the chicken and push the lemon halves into the cavity. Turn in the marinade several times to coat, cover with plastic wrap and refrigerate for several hours or overnight.

Preheat oven to 400F (205C). Place the chicken on a rack in a roasting dish, pour over the marinade and roast for 1-1/2 hours or until the juices run clear when the thigh is pierced with a skewer.

Meanwhile, make the sauce. Place the saffron in a small bowl and add the hot water. Let stand at least 20 minutes or until needed.

Add egg yolks, garlic, lemon juice and saffron and its soaking liquid to a food processor or blender. Process until smooth. With the motor running, slowly add the oil through the feed and process until mixture is thick and creamy. Season to taste with salt and pepper. The sauce will not be as thick as mayonnaise. Chop egg whites into pea-sized pieces and stir into the sauce.

Carve the chicken into serving pieces and serve immediately, with the sauce on the side.

Eggplant Stuffed with Tomato and Saffron

With their crisp, golden tops and smooth, aromatic interiors, these eggplants go well with a beef or pork roast. Don't waste the drained tomato juices; they're full of flavor and goodness, and make a delicious, healthful drink, or add them to soup or stock for a risotto.

MAKES 4 SIDE-DISH SERVINGS

1 lb. (500g) tomatoes, peeled, seeded and roughly chopped

1/4 teaspoon saffron threads

1 tablespoon hot water

2 eggplants, 1 lb. (500g) each

Salt and black pepper

3 tablespoons extra-virgin olive oil

2 cloves garlic, finely chopped

2 tablespoons chopped fresh flat-leaf parsley

6 tablespoons fresh breadcrumbs

Preheat oven to 425F (220C). Lightly oil a baking dish.

Place the tomatoes in a colander and drain 30 minutes. Place the saffron in a small bowl and add the hot water. Let stand at least 20 minutes or until needed. Cut the eggplants in half lengthwise and score around the inside within 1/4 inch (0.6cm) of the skin to make a border. Slash the centers three times diagonally for even cooking.

Transfer to baking dish, season with salt and drizzle with 1 tablespoon of the oil.

Bake 20 minutes or until tender when tested with a skewer. Remove from the oven and, cool slightly to handle, scoop out flesh, leaving 1/4-inch-thick (0.6cm) shells, and chop the flesh roughly.

Heat 1 tablespoon oil in a frying pan over medium heat. Add drained tomatoes and cook, stirring frequently, until dry, about 5 minutes. Add saffron and its soaking liquid, and cook 1 minute. Transfer mixture to a bowl, add chopped eggplant, garlic and parsley. Season well with salt and pepper and spoon into eggplant shells. Sprinkle with breadcrumbs and drizzle with the remaining 1 tablespoon of oil.

Bake 20 minutes or until the tops are golden and crisp. Serve hot, warm or at room temperature.

Garlic

The Earthy

Garlic, a member of the fragrant *Allium* genus, which includes leeks, onions, chives and golden shallots, has not always been embraced as wholeheartedly as it is today. An old Turkish legend claims that when the Devil was banned from Paradise and first set foot on earth, in the place of his left footstep an onion sprang up and, in the right, a garlic bulb.

For their part, the people of the Middle East certainly recognized the health-giving potential of this vegetable. The Egyptian slaves building the great pyramids were sustained by a constant diet of garlic, and in 430 BC the father of medicine, Hippocrates, observed garlic to be the mainstay of the Greek diet of the time, along with onion, cabbages, peas and lentils. Greek warriors were given garlic before going into battle, and to this day bullfighters carry a clove of garlic on their person to prevent the bull from charging. On the other hand, garlic was also seen as an aphrodisiac, and the Brahmins in India refuse to eat garlic or onion because they consider them lust-provoking.

Garlic contains *allyl disulfate*, a natural antiseptic, and *cycloallin*, an anticoagulant that inhibits the formation of clots in blood vessels, thus being a considerable antidote against heart disease and strokes. Garlic also lowers blood cholesterol and facilitates the absorption of vitamins. Cooking does not destroy these powerful properties.

When it comes to cooking with garlic, I find there's absolutely no need for extra equipment, least of all the dreaded garlic press, which renders the garlic moist and the flavor acrid when cooked. If a whole, utterly pristine clove is what you want, blanch the clove with the skin on in a little boiling water. The skin will just slip off. To peel a clove for chopping, lay it on a chopping board and press on it gently with the flat blade of a chef's knife and the skin will come off easily. To chop, simply place the peeled cloves on a board and use a chef's knife with a rocking motion, without the tip of the knife ever leaving the board. To mash garlic into a purée, place whole cloves in a mortar or a bowl on a little salt to keep the garlic in place, and mash with a pestle or the back of a fork or spoon. And for goodness sake, don't worry about garlic smell on your hands—there are certainly many worse smells to worry about!

The flavor of garlic can change dramatically according to the preparation method. Just one small clove, when uncooked, delivers a powerful punch, whereas whole garlic bulbs, roasted in the oven, or garlic cooked slowly in oil, are rendered meltingly tender with a mellow flavor to match.

The French and Italians have wonderful little flavoring aids, which they use extensively to pep up otherwise bland dishes. French *persillade* is a mixture of chopped parsley and garlic, sprinkled onto all manner of foods just before serving, such as cooked vegetables, especially fried potatoes or meats. Italian *gremolata* is a blend of chopped parsley, garlic and lemon zest, without which osso buco wouldn't be complete.

The great French gastronome Marcel Boulestin said, "It's not an exaggeration to say that peace and happiness begin, geographically, where garlic is used in cooking." History may not always support the theory, but I agree with the sentiment.

Recipes

Tarator
Sauce

A simple sauce for true garlic believers, and what a sauce! Originally from Turkey, it's made much the same way as mayonnaise, with the pounded garlic taking the place of egg, and the oil turning the sauce the palest of pale avocado colors. Serve this heady, addictive sauce with any kind of fish, with hot boiled potatoes, or stir cubed, boiled potatoes, still hot, into the sauce for a quick, garlicky potato salad.

MAKES ABOUT 1/2 CUP (120ML)

8 large cloves garlic, peeled and roughly chopped

1/2 teaspoon salt

1/4 cup (60ml) extra-virgin olive oil

Juice of 1/2 lemon

Pinch of hot paprika

Combine the garlic and salt in a mortar and pound with a pestle until you have a smooth paste. Transfer the paste to a bowl and start adding the oil, drop by drop at first, whisking constantly, until you have a sauce of a thick mayonnaise consistency. Whisk in the lemon juice and paprika. Check the seasoning, adding more salt or lemon juice to your own taste. Cover and refrigerate until ready to use. Keeps in refrigerator up to 5 days.

Tzatziki

Despite the fact that this classic sauce or dip contains only one clove of garlic, the flavor is powerful because the garlic remains uncooked. Many versions of this versatile sauce exist all along the Eastern Mediterranean, from Greece, where it's called tzatziki, to Turkey, where it is known as cacik. Serve with crisped pide (Turkish flatbread) or pita bread, corn chips, raw vegetables, in salads or with grilled fish, poultry or meat.

MAKES ABOUT 1 CUP (230ML)

2 English cucumbers or 1 medium regular cucumber

1/4 teaspoon salt

1 clove garlic, peeled

3/4 cup (175ml) plain low-fat yogurt

1 tablespoon extra-virgin olive oil

1 teaspoon red wine vinegar

2 tablespoons finely chopped fresh parsley or mint

Peel the cucumbers, cut in halves lengthwise and remove the seeds with a teaspoon. Finely chop the flesh and set aside to drain in a sieve 20 minutes.

Combine salt and garlic in a mortar or bowl and crush to a smooth paste with a pestle or the back of a spoon. Stir in yogurt, oil, vinegar and parsley, and beat until smooth. Stir in reserved cucumber, cover with plastic wrap and chill until ready to serve. Keeps in refrigerator 1 day.

Garlic and Parmesan Focaccia

Well-made fresh bread is one of my passions, and thanks to the proliferation of good bakeries I now can freely indulge it. It's hard to believe that only a few years ago I had to set aside whole weekends to make the bread I liked to eat. The starter (biga) was made on the first night and put to rest, but going out to lunch or the movies and having dinner on the following day had to be arranged around first rising, second rising and finally baking. Thankfully, enterprising bakers everywhere started baking wood-fired loaves, which were as good as (and to be honest, probably much better than) my own efforts.

But every now and then I get the urge to take out the baking stones and the peel (a flat, shovel-like tool used to slide pizzas and breads in and out of the oven), heat the oven to a good, hot temperature, and again smell the incomparable, yeasty fragrance of baking bread. After much experimentation, I've developed this simple, one-bowl dough recipe, which takes only minutes to make in a electric mixer with a dough hook. The dough may be made into loaves or, as here, into focaccia, which is fabulous as a snack or with drinks.

There's always the question of letting the dough rise in a warm place. It took me a while to find out that the closet where our water heater is housed is a good, warm, draft-free place. So is a laundry with a dryer running, or a gas oven with just the pilot light on. Unglazed terra-cotta tiles make good baking stones and are available wherever tiles are sold. Allow at least a 1/3-inch (1cm) space between the tiles and the oven wall, so air can circulate. A peel is handy to transfer focacce to and from the oven. If you don't have one, use an upside-down baking sheet. I like to use polenta on the peel: The individual grains act like little ball bearings and the focaccia/bread/pizza slides off effortlessly.

Focaccia

3-1/4 cups (760ml) all-purpose flour
or 2-1/2 cups (460ml) all-purpose
flour and 3/4 cup (175ml) whole-
wheat flour

1 teaspoon dry yeast or 1-1/2
teaspoons rapid-rise yeast

1 teaspoon salt

1/2 teaspoon sugar

1 tablespoon extra-virgin olive oil

1 cup (230ml) warm water

Polenta or cornmeal

Garlic and Parmesan Topping

3 tablespoons extra-virgin olive oil

1 onion, halved and thinly sliced

4 cloves garlic, finely sliced
lengthwise

2 teaspoons fresh oregano leaves

Coarse sea salt and black pepper

2 oz./60g (1/3 cup) freshly grated
Parmesan cheese

To make the focaccia: Combine dry ingredients in a heavy-duty electric mixer bowl, add oil and water, and mix until combined. Change to dough hook and knead 10 minutes. Divide dough in half and roll into two balls. Flatten slightly and place on a floured baking sheet. Cover with a damp cloth towel and let rise in a warm place until double in size, about 2 hours when using regular yeast; about 1 hour when using rapid-rise yeast.

Meanwhile, make the topping. Combine oil and onion in a frying pan and cook until soft, stirring frequently, about 5 minutes. Add garlic and cook, stirring, 1 minute. Remove from heat and season with oregano and salt and pepper to taste. Set aside to cool.

Preheat oven, with the baking stones installed, to 425F (220C).

On a generously floured surface, roll dough, one ball at a time, until you have 2 (8-inch/20cm) circles. Transfer focacce to a baking sheet sprinkled with polenta. Spread the onion mixture on top of the focacce, leaving a 3/4-inch (2cm) border. With floured fingers, make indentations all over the surface. Let rise in a draft-free place 45 to 60 minutes. Transfer to a peel or upside-down baking sheet sprinkled with polenta. Sprinkle baking stones with polenta and slide focacce into the oven. Bake 20 minutes, then sprinkle with cheese and bake 10 minutes more, or until tops are golden. Serve at once.

Soft Garlic Potato Purée with Poached Eggs

A deliciously different starter, perfect to kick off a dinner with friends or family, and guaranteed to earn you raves. The consistency of the purée has to be just right, not too stiff, semi-liquid, and the eggs need to be poached at the last minute, with the whites just set and slightly runny yolks.

MAKES 4 FIRST-COURSE SERVINGS

2 heads garlic

About 3/4 lb. (360g) waxy potatoes

4 tablespoons extra-virgin olive oil

Salt and black pepper

Hot water

2 tablespoons white wine vinegar

4 large eggs

2 tablespoons chopped fresh chives

Preheat oven to 375F (190C).

Cut the top 1/3 inch (1cm) off the heads of garlic, so the tops of the cloves are exposed. Drizzle each head with 1 teaspoon of the oil, wrap securely in foil and bake for 30 minutes, or until tender when pressed.

Meanwhile, cook potatoes in their skins until tender. Purée in a ricer, grate, or mash. Add remaining oil, squeeze soft garlic from the bulb into the purée by holding it in one hand and squeezing hard. Season with salt and pepper. Stir in a little hot water to make the purée easily spoonable.

To poach eggs, bring a wide, shallow pan of water to a boil, add vinegar and reduce the heat, so the water shivers. Break each egg, into a cup and slide into the water. Cook until whites are set 3 to 5 minutes. Remove with a slotted spoon and drain briefly, in the spoon, on a folded paper towel. Spoon potato purée into 4 heated plates and place a poached egg in the middle of each. Sprinkle with chives and serve immediately.

Brandade
of Fresh Salmon

This recipe is a radical departure from the original Provençal brandade de morue: *There's no salted or dried fish, simply a fresh piece of salmon, lightly poached and mixed with garlic, potato and oil. The purée is pure delight when served in a rustic bowl as a topping for bruschetta or crostini. Olives are a good accompaniment.*

MAKES 6 FIRST-COURSE SERVINGS

1 (8-oz./240g) skinless, boned salmon fillet

1 (8-oz./240g) baking potato, peeled and cut into 1/3-inch (1cm) cubes

4 cloves garlic, peeled and halved

1/2 cup (120ml) extra-virgin olive oil

1 tablespoon chopped fresh thyme leaves

1-1/2 tablespoons lemon juice

Salt and black pepper

Pour just enough water in a saucepan to cover the fish. Bring it to a simmer, add the salmon and simmer 5 minutes or until salmon is just cooked. Remove to a plate and keep warm. Add potato and garlic to the pan and simmer 12 to 15 minutes. Drain and return to pan, set over medium heat and dry out the potato and garlic, shaking the pan, about 20 seconds.

Meanwhile, combine oil and thyme in a frying pan and set over low heat to warm.

Place the warm potato and garlic in a bowl and beat with an electric mixer (not a food processor) at medium speed until smooth. Crumble salmon, add it to the potato and garlic, and beat until well mixed. Do not use a food processor, which turns the mixture to glue. With mixer running, add warm oil and thyme in a steady trickle, then add lemon juice and season to taste with salt and pepper. Serve immediately.

Garlic Custards

A gorgeous, creamy starter with an unforgettable mellow garlic flavor and velvety texture. Purists would season these little custards with white pepper, but I like the little black flecks, like real vanilla in ice cream or custard.

MAKES 4 FIRST-COURSE SERVINGS

1 head garlic

1 teaspoon extra-virgin olive oil

2 large eggs, plus 1 egg yolk, lightly beaten

1/2 cup (120ml) light cream

1 cup (230ml) whole milk

Salt and black pepper

Lightly dressed salad greens, such as arugula or watercress, to serve

Preheat oven to 375F (190C).

Cut the top 1/3 inch (1cm) off the head of garlic, so the tops of the cloves are exposed. Drizzle with 1 teaspoon oil, wrap securely in foil and bake 30 minutes, or until tender when pressed. Let cool enough to handle and squeeze the soft garlic from the bulb into a mortar or bowl by holding it in one hand and squeezing hard. Mash to a paste with a pestle or fork. Reduce oven temperature to 300F (150C).

Meanwhile, beat together eggs, cream and milk. Stir cooled purée into egg mixture; force the combination through a strainer. Season with salt and pepper; divide among 4 buttered, 1/2-cup (120ml) molds or ramekins.

Place molds in a baking dish, place in the oven and fill the dish with very hot water to halfway up the sides of the molds. Bake 35 minutes, or until set when a mold is shaken. Remove from oven and allow to stand in hot water bath 10 minutes more.

To serve, line 4 plates with salad greens. Run a sharp knife around the insides of molds; turn the custards out onto the greens. Serve immediately.

Garlic and Chive
Bread and Butter Puddings

A great starter, light lunch or supper, these puddings may be prepared well ahead of time. The golden, crisp bits on top always seem to be the most desirable; to get more crunch and less sogginess, make these in shallow dishes, such as small oval or round gratins. Alternatively, a large, 1-1/2 quart (1.5 liters) baking dish may be used.

MAKES 8 FIRST-COURSE OR LIGHT MAIN-DISH SERVINGS

1 head garlic

1 teaspoon extra-virgin olive oil

1/4 cup/60g (2 oz.) unsalted butter, at room temperature

10 thick slices Italian-style white bread, crusts discarded, cut into 1/3-inch (1cm) cubes

5 large eggs

3 cups milk

Salt and black pepper

1 small bunch fresh chives, snipped

2/3 cup (60g) freshly grated Parmesan cheese, plus 2 tablespoons for top

2 tablespoons butter, chopped

Preheat oven to 375F (190C).

Cut the top 1/3 inch (1cm) off the head of garlic, exposing the cloves. Drizzle with the oil, wrap in foil and bake 30 minutes, or until tender when pressed. Let cool enough to handle. holding the bulb in one hand, press the soft garlic into a large bowl containing the soft butter. With a fork, stir into a smooth paste.

Add bread cubes and mix well. Reduce oven temperature to 300F (150C).

Beat eggs in a bowl with the milk, season with salt and pepper, stir in chives and Parmesan. Pour over bread cubes, mix well and let stand 1 hour. Transfer to 8 (3/4-cup/175ml) baking dishes, dot with butter, sprinkle with remaining cheese and place dishes in a baking pan. Fill the baking pan with hot water halfway up the sides of the baking dishes; bake 40 to 50 minutes until golden and custard has set. Serve immediately.

Bruschetta with Parmesan, Pancetta and Garlic

A delicious nibble to accompany drinks, something you can rustle up in a few minutes. A big wedge of Parmesan cheese is always in my refrigerator, and pancetta, in small packages, in the freezer, ready to be defrosted when I suddenly decide to use it in pasta sauces, risotto, or as in this topping. Don't be tempted to add salt; the cheese and pancetta contribute enough.

MAKES ABOUT 32 HORS D'OEUVRE

6 cloves garlic, peeled

4 oz. (120g) Parmesan cheese, cut into small cubes

4 oz. (120g) pancetta, chopped

2 tablespoons fresh rosemary leaves

1/4 cup (60ml) flat-leaf parsley

3 tablespoons extra-virgin olive oil

8 thick slices Italian-style bread, such as ciabatta

Preheat the broiler.

With the motor running, drop the garlic through the feed tube of a food processor or blender and pulse until finely chopped. Add the cheese, pancetta, rosemary and parsley, and pulse until finely chopped. With the motor running, add the oil in a steady stream. Set aside.

Grill the bread on one side only until golden brown. Turn over and spread the uncooked side with the garlic mixture. Return to the broiler, and cook until the topping is fragrant and golden brown. Cut into large, bite-sized pieces and serve while hot.

Potato, Garlic and Greens Soup

(Caldo Verde)

This addictive soup (caldo verde means green soup) is Portugal's national dish, and you only need one mouthful to understand why. A good amount of fresh cilantro shows the North African influence, but if you don't like this herb you can leave it out or replace it with basil or parsley. In Portugal, this soup is made with couve, a native cabbage, or kale; people can be seen cutting huge bunches in the fields for their midday caldo verde.

MAKES 6 FIRST-COURSE OR 4 MAIN-COURSE SERVINGS

2 tablespoons extra-virgin olive oil, plus extra for servings

2 baking potatoes (1-1/4 lbs./600g total), peeled and cut into cubes

2 cloves garlic, finely chopped

4-3/4 cups (1.1 liters) water

Salt

6-1/2 oz. (200g) finely shredded green leaves, such as green cabbage, spinach or Swiss chard

4 tablespoons chopped cilantro

2 oz. (60g) very thinly sliced cooked sausage, such as chorizo

Combine the oil, potatoes and garlic in a pan and stir over medium heat until thoroughly coated in the oil, 3 to 4 minutes. Add 2 cups (460ml) of the water and a little salt, and bring to a boil. Cover and simmer until the potatoes are tender, 12 to 15 minutes, depending on size of the cubes.

Mash the potatoes into the liquid and add the remaining water. Bring to a simmer, add the greens and cilantro, and cook 12 minutes only, making sure the greens don't become limp. Serve in heated bowls and float a few wafer-thin slices of sausage on top. Pass olive oil for diners to drizzle into their soup.

Summer Vegetable Soup with Garlic and Rice

Similar to the Spanish gazpacho, this refreshing soup is ideal when you're on summer vacation in a rented house. A food processor is not necessary because all the ingredients are chopped by hand. Whenever we go to our favorite seaside destination, I pack a basket with my chef's knife, a bread knife, a small paring knife and a carving knife. Of course, there are several other essentials, like a knife sharpener, a corkscrew and pepper and salt mills. The garlic in this soup is actually removed after flavoring the fragrant mixture.

MAKES 4 FIRST-COURSE SERVINGS

1 red onion, chopped

2 English cucumbers, peeled, seeded and cut into pea-sized cubes

1 red or yellow red bell pepper, cut into pea-sized cubes

6 large cloves garlic, bruised with the flat side of a chef's knife, but left in one piece

6 large, ripe tomatoes, peeled, seeded and finely chopped

1/3 cup (80ml) arborio rice, cooked

3 tablespoons extra-virgin olive oil

1 tablespoon red wine vinegar

2 cups (460ml) water

Hot pepper sauce

Salt and black pepper

About 1/4 cup (60ml) fresh basil, torn into pieces, plus extra for garnish

Crusty bread, to serve

Combine all the ingredients, except for the garnish and bread, in a bowl and stir well. Cover with plastic wrap and refrigerate at least 4 hours. Just before serving, remove the garlic cloves, check the seasoning and sprinkle with some basil. Serve with plenty of bread.

Lentil and Pasta Soup

Use only brown or green lentils for this soup. The red variety doesn't hold its shape and turns into mush. Try to find the tiniest lentils, such as the slate-colored French lentilles vertes du Puy, *which have superior flavor and texture. I admit they're outrageously expensive, but are well worth the price for a special occasion. I like to serve this soup to people who are coming in from the cold, for comforting and nourishing sustenance.*

MAKES 6 LIGHT MAIN-COURSE OR
4 MAIN-COURSE SERVINGS

1 cup (230ml) lentils

2 oz. (60g) pancetta, cubed

1 small onion, finely chopped

4 cloves garlic, finely chopped

1 fresh hot red chile, thinly sliced

1 large carrot, cut into tiny cubes

1 stalk celery, cut into tiny cubes

3 tablespoons chopped parsley

2 tablespoons extra-virgin olive oil

3/4 cup (175ml) dry white wine

4-3/4 cups (1.1 liters) water

5 oz. (150g) small pasta shapes,
   such as ditoli or tubetti

Salt and black pepper

Freshly grated Parmesan cheese
   and extra-virgin olive oil, to serve

Place the lentils in a bowl and add enough warm water to cover by 2 inches (5cm). Set aside for 30 minutes.

Meanwhile, combine the pancetta, onion, garlic, chile, carrot, celery, 2 tablespoons of the parsley and the oil in a large Dutch oven. Cook until vegetables are soft, about 15 minutes, stirring frequently.

Drain the lentils, add them to the Dutch oven and cook 5 minutes, stirring frequently. Add the wine and water, bring to a simmer and cover. Simmer 25 to 30 minutes, or until the lentils are tender. Add pasta and cook until tender, 5 to 8 minutes. Season to taste with salt and pepper, sprinkle with parsley, and serve immediately in heated deep bowls. Pass Parmesan cheese and olive oil separately at the table.

Green Minestrone

As a food writer, I see many and varied articles and produce come my way. When a bountiful basket with the best of the spring vegetables arrived, it happened to be one of these rare weeks when I had to go out every night. Come the weekend, and I decided to do something befitting them; this green minestrone is the happy result.

MAKES 6 FIRST-COURSE OR LIGHT MAIN-DISH SERVINGS

1 cup (230ml) cannellini beans, soaked

2 tablespoons extra-virgin olive oil

2 large onions, thickly sliced

4 cloves garlic, finely chopped

1/2 bunch celery, sliced

2 medium potatoes, peeled and cut into bite-sized cubes

4 artichokes, trimmed and quartered (see page 89)

1 bunch asparagus, woody ends snapped off and discarded, cut diagonally into 1-3/4-inch (4cm) pieces

1 lb. (500g) fresh fava beans, shelled

8 oz. (240g) sugar snap peas, cut diagonally into 1/3-inch (1cm) pieces

6 cups (1.4 liters) chicken stock

Salt and black pepper

1 bunch arugula, chopped

Drain soaked beans and rinse well. Return to the pan, cover with water, and bring to a simmer. Simmer until the beans are tender, 40 to 60 minutes; drain. Meanwhile, combine oil and onions in a Dutch oven and cook until soft, stirring frequently, 5 minutes. Add garlic and cook, stirring, 1 minute.

Add celery, potatoes and artichokes and stir to coat them with the oil, then stir in the asparagus, fava beans and sugar snap peas.

Stir in chicken stock, adding water if necessary to cover all vegetables, and season with salt and pepper. Simmer 15 minutes. Stir in cannellini beans and cook 10 minutes more, until vegetables are tender. Stir in the arugula, cook 1 minute, or until it wilts, and serve immediately.

Pasta for Summer with Arugula, Tomatoes, Garlic and Oil

In the warmer weather, I hardly ever let a weekend lunch pass without making this delicious pasta. As far as I'm concerned, the more garlic, the better. The tomatoes and arugula stay uncooked; only the oil, garlic and chile are set over a very low heat to infuse the oil with heady aroma. I always remove the chiles before serving, and the garlic could be strained from the oil as well, but why not eat it—the slow cooking renders it meltingly tender and sweet; in fact, it becomes a garlic confit.

MAKE 4 LIGHT MAIN-DISH SERVINGS

1/4 cup (60ml) extra-virgin olive oil

8 cloves garlic, chopped

4 to 8 fresh hot red chiles, split, stem left attached

2 large bunches arugula

6 medium or 4 large tomatoes

Salt and black pepper

1 lb. (500g) linguine or other long, dried pasta

Combine the oil, garlic and chiles in a small frying pan and place over low heat so an occasional bubble breaks the surface. The garlic should not change color. Use a heat diffuser if necessary.

Rinse the arugula and shake dry or spin in a salad spinner. Remove lower stems and chop leaves and tender stems. Place in a shallow bowl.

Chop the tomatoes roughly, season to taste with salt and add to the arugula. Toss well and set aside.

Meanwhile, cook the pasta in boiling, salted water until al dente, then drain. Add to the bowl, quickly remove the chiles from the oil and pour the oil and garlic over the pasta. Toss well, grind black pepper over the top and serve immediately.

Pasta for Winter with Radicchio, Potatoes, Garlic and Oil

This is a cold-weather variation on the previous pasta, sharing equal top billing in my household. Potatoes are not an uncommon addition to pasta; the original fettuccine alla Genovese *(with pesto) always contains potatoes and green beans, cooked along with the pasta. In this dish, the seductive combination of the bitter leaves, the bland potatoes bathed in garlicky, peppery oil and pasta makes this another runaway favorite. I strongly advocate not removing the core from the radicchio; its inclusion lends the dish an interesting texture.*

MAKE 4 LIGHT MAIN-DISH SERVINGS

6 tablespoons extra-virgin olive oil

8 cloves garlic, chopped

4 to 8 fresh hot red chiles, split, stem left attached

1 lb. (500g) potatoes, peeled

12 oz. (360g) long, dried pasta, such as fettuccine or spaghetti

1 large or 2 small firm head(s) radicchio, cut into quarters, then cut across into strips

Combine the oil, garlic and chiles in a small frying pan and place over low heat so an occasional bubble in the oil breaks the surface. The garlic should not change color. Use a heat diffuser if necessary.

Cut the potatoes into 1/2-inch (1cm) cubes. Set aside in a bowl, covered with water.

Bring a large pot of salted water to a boil. Add potatoes and bring water to a boil, cook 2 minutes, then add pasta. Cook until pasta is al dente and potatoes are tender, 8 to 10 minutes, stirring occasionally. Add radicchio to the pot, stir just until wilted, 30 to 60 seconds; drain immediately.

Transfer pasta mixture to a heated bowl, remove chiles from the oil and pour oil and garlic over pasta and vegetables. Toss well and serve immediately.

Pasta with Cabbage, Garlic and Bacon

Cabbage in a pasta sauce may sound surprising, but when you try this version I'm sure you'll find it surprisingly good. Yet another example of how, in peasant cuisines, literally everything is put to good use, and then, with just a few simple ingredients added, made sublime.

MAKES 6 FIRST-COURSE OR 4 MAIN-COURSE SERVINGS

1 (1-lb./500g) cabbage head, cut into 4 equal wedges

1/4 cup (60ml) extra-virgin olive oil

6 oz. (180g) lean bacon or ham, cut into narrow strips

8 cloves garlic, coarsely chopped

1/4 teaspoon hot chile flakes (optional)

Salt and black pepper

1 lb. (500g) pasta, such as linguine or tagliatelle

Freshly grated Parmesan cheese

Plunge the cabbage wedges into a pot of lightly salted, boiling water and cook until the core is tender, about 10 minutes. Drain and set aside to cool. When cool, chop roughly.

Meanwhile, combine the oil and bacon in a frying pan and cook until bacon is crisp. Remove with a slotted spoon and drain. Reduce heat to low, add garlic and cook 6 to 8 minutes until light golden. Remove the garlic and set aside.

Increase the heat under the oil to medium-high, add the cabbage and cook, tossing frequently, until starting to color, 10 minutes. Return the garlic and cook for 1 minute more to blend the flavors.

Meanwhile, cook the pasta in boiling, salted water until al dente. Drain and transfer to a heated bowl. Add cabbage and reserved bacon, toss well and serve immediately. Serve with Parmesan cheese.

Pasta with Mussels in a Piquant Tomato Sauce

When taking mussels from the shell after cooking, you'll often find little crabs inside, which Waverley Root in his definitive book, Food, *calls* mussel crabs, *and Stephanie Alexander in her wonderful book,* The Cook's Companion, *identifies as* soldier crabs. *In any case, they're a charming, crunchy addition to any dish, so to do them justice, eat them and don't throw them out.*

MAKES 4 LIGHT MAIN-DISH SERVINGS

4 lb. (2kg) black mussels

2 tablespoons extra-virgin olive oil

2 cloves garlic, finely chopped

4 tablespoons finely chopped fresh flat-leaf parsley

2 fresh hot red chiles, chopped (remove seeds, if desired)

1-1/4 lb. (625g) plum tomatoes, seeded and chopped

3 tablespoons dry white wine

Salt and black pepper

12 oz. (360g) long, dried pasta, such as linguine or spaghetti

Soak the mussels in a sinkful of water for 1 hour. Scrub if necessary and pull off the beards. Place in a pan, cover and place over high heat, shaking the pan vigorously from time to time.

The mussels should all open within 5 minutes; discard any that haven't. Remove mussels from pan and remove mussels from their shells. Set mussels aside and strain the cooking water and reserve.

Combine the oil, garlic, 2 tablespoons parsley and chiles in a deep frying pan. Cook over medium-low heat until aromatic, stirring frequently, about 3 minutes. Add tomatoes, wine and reserved mussel liquid; cook until sauce reduces and thickens, 12 to 15 minutes. Add mussels, season with salt and pepper and keep warm over low heat.

Meanwhile, cook pasta in boiling, salted water until al dente. Drain and add to tomato mixture. Toss over medium heat 2 minutes and serve immediately, sprinkled with remaining parsley.

Risotto with Artichokes and Asparagus

This risotto spells "springtime," just as mushrooms are synonymous with autumn and luscious tomatoes will forever be associated with summer. Cooked this way, the silvery-gray artichokes are combined in a perfect risotto, with crunchy bright green asparagus tips for color.

MAKES 6 FIRST-COURSE OR 4 LIGHT MAIN-COURSE SERVINGS

6 cups (1.4 liters) chicken stock

8 oz. (240g) asparagus, trimmed, 2-inch (6cm) tips cut off and reserved, remaining stalks cut into 1/3-inch (1cm) lengths

3 tablespoons extra-virgin olive oil

1 large red onion, chopped

4 cloves garlic, finely chopped

4 artichokes, trimmed (see page 89) and cut into 1/3-inch (1cm) wedges

2 cups (360g) arborio rice

3/4 cup (175ml) dry white wine

Salt and black pepper

2 oz./60g (2/3 cup) freshly grated Parmesan cheese

2 tablespoons chopped parsley

Bring chicken stock to a boil, add asparagus tips, return to a boil and cook about 2 minutes. Remove and rinse under cold water. Drain and reserve. Reduce heat until stock simmers.

Combine oil and onion in a heavy saucepan and cook until onion is soft, stirring frequently, 5 minutes. Add garlic and cook, stirring, 1 minute more. Add asparagus stalks, artichokes and rice, and cook, stirring, to coat with oil, 2 minutes. Pour in wine and cook, stirring, until absorbed. Add a ladleful of the simmering stock, and stir until liquid is absorbed. Continue adding stock, making sure the stock has been absorbed before adding more. Cook 20 to 25 minutes. Season lightly with salt and pepper about halfway through the cooking time. If stock runs out, add simmering water. Reserve a few tablespoons of stock to add last.

Stir in reserved stock, asparagus tips, Parmesan cheese and parsley. Stir vigorously, cover pan and let stand 3 minutes. Serve in heated deep plates.

Garlic Risotto

Especially for garlic lovers, this delicious risotto delivers a triple whammy. The first batch of garlic is thinly sliced, then fried until golden and crisp to sprinkle on top at the end, making garlic-flavored oil in the process; the second is baked in the oven until meltingly tender and mashed to be stirred in at the last moment. Not overpowering at all; on the contrary, as demure and sweet as jasmine in springtime. I like to serve this as a starter to a light meal, or as the main event for lunch, accompanied by a salad. Make sure you're feeding garlic fanatics when serving this.

MAKES 6 FIRST-COURSE OR 4 LIGHT MAIN-COURSE SERVINGS

2 heads garlic

2 teaspoons extra-virgin olive oil

Risotto

3 tablespoons extra-virgin olive oil

8 cloves garlic, peeled, sliced

1 onion, chopped

4 oz. (120g) pancetta, chopped

1-3/4 cups (360g) arborio rice

3/4 cup (175ml) dry white wine

6 cups (1.4 liters) chicken stock, simmering

Salt and black pepper

4 oz./120g (1-1/3 cups) freshly grated Parmesan cheese

2 tablespoons chopped fresh parsley

Preheat oven to 375F (190C).

Slice off the top 1/3 inch (1cm) of each garlic head, exposing the cloves, drizzle each one with 1 teaspoon of the oil and wrap securely in foil. Bake 30 minutes, or until the garlic is soft when pressed. Let cool enough to handle. Holding the whole bulb in one hand, squeeze the cloves into a bowl. Mash with a fork until smooth and set aside.

To make the risotto, combine oil and thinly sliced garlic in a heavy saucepan, and cook over medium-low heat until garlic is golden and crisp, about 5 minutes. Remove with a slotted spoon; set aside, drain on paper towels.

Add onion to the pan and cook over medium heat until soft, stirring frequently, about 5 minutes. Add pancetta and cook 5 minutes more, stirring frequently. Add rice and stir 2 minutes, until all the rice is coated with oil. Add wine and stir until absorbed, about 2 minutes. Start adding the simmering stock one ladleful at a time, adding another ladle when the previous one has been absorbed. Cook 20 to 25 minutes. Season lightly with salt and pepper about halfway through the cooking time. If the stock runs out, add simmering water.

Reserve a few tablespoons of the stock to add last.

Stir in reserved garlic purée and stock, and stir vigorously 1 minute. Stir in Parmesan cheese and parsley, cover the pan and let stand 3 minutes before serving. Serve the reserved crisp garlic in a separate bowl at the table.

Chickpeas with Chicory and Cumin

This is a treasured chickpea recipe, redolent of earthy cumin, a good dose of garlic, the slight bitterness of chicory, which may be replaced with Swiss chard or spinach, a modest touch of chile and a generous splash of lemon juice. It is paradise on earth for bean lovers. It's virtually impossible to overcook chickpeas and during the second stage of their cooking they absorb the delicious flavors without becoming mushy or losing texture.

MAKES 4 MAIN-COURSE OR 6 TO 8
SIDE-DISH SERVINGS

12 oz. (360g) chickpeas, soaked

1 tablespoon cumin seeds

2 tablespoons extra-virgin olive oil

2 red onions, roughly chopped

4 large cloves garlic, chopped

Juice of 1 large lemon

1/2 teaspoon hot chile flakes

1 bunch chicory or Swiss chard
  stemmed and chopped

Salt and black pepper

Drain soaked chickpeas, place in a saucepan and cover with water (no salt). Bring to a boil. Reduce heat, cover and simmer 1 hour, or until chickpeas are tender. Strain and reserve the cooking liquid.

Meanwhile, place cumin seeds in a small, dry frying pan and roast over medium heat, shaking the pan frequently, until they are aromatic and begin to color. Cool slightly and pulverize with a pestle in a mortar. Set aside.

Combine oil and onions in a heavy saucepan and cook until soft, stirring frequently, about 5 minutes. Add cumin and garlic and cook, stirring, 1 minute. Add drained chickpeas, lemon juice, chile flakes and reserved cooking liquid to barely cover. Bring to a simmer, cover and cook 45 minutes over low heat. Stir in chicory, season with salt and pepper, cover and simmer until tender, 15 minutes. Serve in heated deep plates.

Garlic Baby Calamari

If people only knew how easy calamari (squid) are to clean and prepare for cooking, they would eat a whole lot more of them. Nothing is easier: Simply pull out the long, dangling tentacles. Push out the hard beak in the center of the tentacles and cut off the head just below the eyes. Pull out the plastic-looking quill and discard. Pull at the flaps, pull off the skin and rinse the body thoroughly, inside and out, removing any foreign material. For this recipe, buy only baby calamari. They'll puff up beguilingly during their short baking.

MAKES 4 FIRST-COURSE SERVINGS

20 baby calamari (squid), 4 to 5 inches (10-12.5 cm) long, cleaned as above

4 large cloves garlic, chopped

5 tablespoons extra-virgin olive oil

3 tablespoons dry white wine

Salt and black pepper

1 teaspoon balsamic vinegar

4 cups young arugula leaves

2 tablespoons chopped parsley

Crusty bread, to serve

Preheat oven to 425F (220C).

Place the calamari in a large baking dish that will hold them in one layer. Toss with the garlic, 2 tablespoons of the oil, the wine and salt and pepper to taste, making sure some of the mixture goes inside the tubes.

Bake 15 minutes, or until the calamari are just cooked through and puffed.

Meanwhile, combine the vinegar and remaining 3 tablespoons oil in a large bowl, add the arugula and toss the arugula in the mixture with your hands, until the bowl is clean and the arugula is lightly dressed. Spread on plates, place the calamari on top and pour over accumulated juices. Sprinkle with parsley and serve immediately.

Swordfish Steaks in Herbed Sauce

This traditional Sicilian recipe is perfect for summer. It's superb when served as soon as it's cooked, but its equally good when made in advance, allowed to cool and served at room temperature. Instead of swordfish, tuna or white firm-fleshed fish fillets such as halibut, snapper or sea bass may be used. Serve with crusty bread.

MAKES 4 MAIN-COURSE SERVINGS

4 swordfish steaks

2 tablespoons extra-virgin olive oil

Salt and black pepper

Salmoriglio (Herbed Olive Oil and Lemon Juice Sauce)

1/2 teaspoon salt

2 cloves garlic

4 tablespoons extra-virgin olive oil

2 tablespoons hot water

2 tablespoons lemon juice

1 tablespoon finely chopped fresh oregano leaves

2 tablespoons chopped parsley

Place fish in a dish, pour over the oil and season lightly with salt and pepper. Turn fish in the oil to coat, cover with plastic wrap and set aside while you make the sauce. Preheat a cast-iron skillet or the barbecue until very hot.

To make the *salmoriglio*, combine the salt and garlic in a mortar or bowl and crush to a smooth paste with a pestle or the back of a spoon. Combine garlic paste with the oil, hot water and lemon juice in a bowl and whisk until thickened. Stir in oregano and parsley.

Grill fish until just cooked through, about 5 minutes, turning once. Immediately place in a dish and baste with the oil-and-herb sauce. Serve at once or let cool to room temperature.

Grilled Fish with Greek Garlic and Walnut Sauce

A firm-fleshed fish, such as swordfish, tuna or halibut, works well for this robust recipe, which is served on a refreshing bed of parsley leaves and thin onion rings.

MAKES 4 MAIN-COURSE SERVINGS

Greek Garlic and Walnut Sauce

1 (6-oz./180g) baking potato

1/2 teaspoon salt

6 cloves garlic, chopped

6 oz. (180g) walnuts, ground

Juice of 1 lemon

1/2 cup (120ml) extra-virgin olive oil

Hot water

4 fish steaks, such as swordfish, tuna or halibut

2 tablespoons extra-virgin olive oil

1 tablespoon lemon juice

2 cloves garlic, finely chopped

1 cup (230ml) chopped parsley

1 red onion, thinly sliced into rings

Crusty bread and lemon wedges, to serve

To make the sauce: Boil the potato in its skin until tender, then peel and mash in a large bowl. Meanwhile, combine salt and garlic in a mortar and grind to a paste. Add garlic to potato, together with the walnuts. Whisk to combine, and stir in lemon juice. Add olive oil a little at a time, whisking constantly. When all oil has been used, whisk in a little hot water until you have a soft, spoonable consistency. Set aside at least 1 hour, to develop the flavors.

Place the fish steaks in a large dish in a single layer. Drizzle oil and lemon juice over fish, and sprinkle with garlic. Turn to coat, cover and set aside; refrigerate if longer than 30 minutes.

Heat a cast-iron skillet, remove fish from marinade, and cook, 2 to 5 minutes each side. Divide parsley among 4 plates. Top each plate with 1/4 of onion rings and 1 fish steak. Serve bread, lemon wedges and sauce separately.

Veal Stew with Garlic, Artichokes and Lima Beans

A springtime stew, in which veal and vegetables are initially cooked separately, comes together in this unbeatable combination of light texture and luscious flavors. The beautiful cooking juices warrant a good loaf of crusty bread to mop up with. To highlight the ethereal aspect of this dish, the juice of a whole lemon is added just before serving.

MAKES 4 MAIN-COURSE SERVINGS

Veal

1 tablespoon extra-virgin olive oil

1-1/2 lb. (750g) veal cubes

1/2 cup (120ml) dry white wine

3/4 cup (175ml) chicken stock

Salt and black pepper

Vegetables

2 tablespoons extra-virgin olive oil

1 red onion, coarsely chopped

4 cloves garlic, finely chopped

2 potatoes, cubed

4 artichokes, trimmed and quartered (see page 89)

1 lb. (500g) fresh peas, shelled (do not use frozen)

1 lb. (500g) Lima beans, shelled

Salt and black pepper

To finish

1 bunch arugula, cut into fine shreds

Juice of 1 lemon

Heat a cast-iron frying pan over high heat. Add oil and, when sizzling, cook veal cubes, in batches, until lightly browned on all sides. Transfer each batch to a Dutch oven. Add wine to the frying pan and bring to a boil, scraping up any browned bits from the bottom. Add stock and return to a boil. Immediately pour over the veal and season to taste with salt and pepper. Bring to a simmer, cover and cook until veal is tender, about 1 hour.

Meanwhile, cook the vegetables. Combine the oil and onion in a heavy saucepan and cook until the onion is soft, stirring frequently, about 5 minutes. Add the garlic and cook, stirring, until aromatic, 1 minute more. Add the potatoes and artichokes, and stir about 2 minutes to coat well with the oil mixture. Stir in peas and beans, and add enough water to just cover. Season to taste with salt and pepper, bring to a simmer and cook gently until the vegetables are tender, about 25 minutes.

Add vegetables and arugula to the veal and simmer 10 minutes more to blend flavors. Stir in lemon juice and serve immediately.

Oregano and Garlic Veal Patties

These veal patties remind me of a summer vacation spent in Sicily. After eating too many sophisticated and heavy meals, this simple but flavorsome dish encapsulated for me all that's so good about the Mediterranean cuisine: basically peasant food, prepared with a light hand and unfailing aptitude for the right combination of flavors. That's what I call chic!

MAKES 4 MAIN-COURSE SERVINGS

1 lb. (500g) lean veal, ground

4 cloves garlic, finely chopped

3 tablespoons fresh breadcrumbs

1 large egg

1 teaspoon small capers, drained

3 teaspoons chopped fresh oregano

Salt and black pepper

2 tablespoons extra-virgin olive oil

1/4 cup (60ml) red wine

1/4 cup (60ml) water

1 large tomato, chopped

3 tablespoons chopped parsley

Combine the veal in a large bowl with the garlic, breadcrumbs, egg, capers and 2 teaspoons oregano. Season to taste with salt and pepper. Shape into 4 equal patties and refrigerate 30 minutes to firm up.

Heat a heavy frying pan over high heat, add oil and cook the patties on both sides until brown, about 4 minutes each side. Transfer to a plate and add the wine, water and remaining oregano to the pan. Cook over high heat, scraping up any browned bits from the bottom, until the liquid is reduced by half. Add the tomato and return the patties to the pan, together with any juices accumulated on the plate. Heat through for 2 minutes then serve immediately, sprinkled with the parsley.

Garlic and Cumin Roasted Lamb

A no-nonsense, totally straightforward lamb roast with fabulous flavor. Try a deboned leg of lamb for easy carving. I like to serve this with roasted potatoes, first parboiled, then halved or quartered and combined in a baking dish with a little olive oil and rosemary. The lamb and potatoes go into the oven together, in separate dishes, and when the lamb is removed, the oven goes up to the highest possible setting to crisp the potatoes while the lamb is resting. Serve with a green salad.

MAKES 4 TO 6 MAIN-COURSE
SERVINGS

10 large cloves garlic, peeled

1 leg of lamb

1 tablespoon cumin seeds

1 teaspoon salt

1 tablespoon extra-virgin olive oil

Preheat oven to 350F (180C).

Cut 5 garlic cloves in half lengthwise and insert into slits made with a sharp knife on all sides of the lamb. Place the cumin seeds in a small dry frying pan over medium heat. Dry-roast the seeds until fragrant. Remove from heat and transfer to a mortar. Add salt and crush with a pestle until finely ground. Add remaining garlic cloves and mash to a paste. Add the oil and combine well.

Using your fingers, spread the paste all over the lamb. Set on a rack in a baking pan. Roast for 20 to 25 minutes per 1 lb. (500g) for rare, or 25 to 30 minutes per 1 lb. (500g) for medium-rare. Remove from the oven, cover the lamb with a tent of foil and let stand for 20 minutes before carving.

Garlic Pot Roast of Beef with Red Wine

Pot-roasting is a method usually reserved for lesser-quality meats, gently simmered for a long period of time. In countries around the Mediterranean, frequently cooks did not have an oven at home, and the Sunday roast would be taken to the baker to cook in the smoldering ashes after he had finished cooking his bread for the day. Á la Boulangre in recipe titles refers to this practice.

MAKES 4 TO 6 MAIN-COURSE SERVINGS

1 (2-lb./1kg) beef tenderloin

Ground black pepper

2 tablespoons extra-virgin olive oil

1 head garlic, cloves separated and peeled

Salt

1/2 cup (120ml) red wine

Rub the beef generously with black pepper, pressing it in well. Place beef in a dish and drizzle 1 tablespoon oil over it, turning several times to coat. Sprinkle garlic around beef and cover with plastic wrap. Set aside at room temperature 20 to 30 minutes, or refrigerate 2 hours or overnight.

Heat a Dutch oven over medium heat, add remaining 1 tablespoon oil and, when hot, add the beef and garlic. Brown beef on all sides and turn garlic cloves frequently. When cloves are golden all over, remove and set aside, but don't discard.

Roast the meat in the Dutch oven 20 to 35 minutes for medium-rare, depending on thickness, turning frequently.

Remove beef from Dutch oven and keep warm. Add wine, increase heat to high and cook, scraping up any browned bits from the bottom. Cook until wine is reduced by half, about 3 minutes. Remove from heat. Season with salt, return beef and garlic, and cover. Let stand, off the heat, 20 minutes. Slice meat and arrange on a heated platter. Spoon over pan juices and garlic, and serve immediately.

Game Hens with Garlic and Lemon Juice

One of the good things about Cornish game hens is their size: Whole, they're big enough for hearty eaters; halved, they're just right for the small-to-average appetite. In this recipe, the hens are first roasted wrapped in foil and, when fully cooked, briefly turned in oil and garlic, and doused with lemon juice. This may not be the most alluring dish, but the succulently tender birds more than make up for the loss of glamour. Serve with roasted potatoes and vegetables, such as fennel or artichokes.

MAKES 4 TO 6 MAIN-COURSE SERVINGS

4 (about 1-lb./500g each) Cornish game hens, thawed if frozen

5 tablespoons extra-virgin olive oil

Salt and black pepper

4 sprigs fresh rosemary

4 cloves garlic, finely chopped

1/2 cup (120ml) lemon juice

1/2 cup (120ml) dry white wine or water

Preheat oven to 400F (200C).

Clean the hens inside and out, removing any fat. Dry hens on paper towels, rub all over with 2 tablespoons oil and season with salt and pepper. Place a sprig of rosemary inside each. Wrap each hen in foil, place in a baking dish.

Roast 1 hour or until juices run clear when pierced in the thigh with a skewer. Remove from the oven and cut hens in half lengthwise.

Combine the remaining 3 tablespoons oil and garlic in a large pan (preferably one large enough to hold the halved hens in one layer), and cook over medium heat, stirring frequently, 3 minutes. Add hens and cook 5 minutes turning occasionally. Add lemon juice and cook 5 minutes more, turning occasionally.

Place hens on a serving platter and keep warm. Add wine or water to the pan and bring to a boil, scraping up any browned bits from the bottom. Boil until the sauce thickens, about 2 minutes, then strain over the hens. Serve immediately.

Chicken with Garlic and Herbs

Forty cloves may seem like an awful lot of garlic, but the way they're sautéed in oil until golden, before they are added to the chicken, makes the whole dish rich with—rather than overpowered—by garlic.

MAKES 4 TO 6 MAIN-COURSE SERVINGS

4 tablespoons extra-virgin olive oil

40 cloves garlic (about 2 heads), peeled, sliced lengthwise

1 (3- to 4-lb./1.5-2kg) chicken or 2 (2-lb./1kg) chickens, cut into serving pieces

Salt and black pepper

1/2 cup (120ml) brandy

1/2 cup (120ml) dry white wine

1 cup (230ml) chicken stock

1 tablespoon chopped fresh thyme leaves

2 teaspoons chopped fresh rosemary leaves

Heat oil in a large Dutch oven. Add garlic and sauté until golden, stirring frequently, 5 to 8 minutes. Remove with a slotted spoon and drain on paper towels.

Rinse chicken with cold water and pat dry with paper towels and season to taste with salt and pepper. Reheat oil in the Dutch oven and sauté chicken over medium heat until golden on all sides. Remove from pan and set aside. Add brandy to pan and cook, scraping up any browned bits from bottom, then add wine, stock, thyme, rosemary and reserved garlic, reserving a few tablespoons of garlic for garnish. Season to taste with salt and pepper, bring to a boil and return chicken to pan. Reduce heat to simmer, cover pan and simmer until chicken is tender, 30 to 40 minutes.

Remove chicken to a heated platter and keep warm. Cook liquids in the pan over high heat until reduced to a sauce-like consistency, then pour over chicken and sprinkle with reserved garlic. Serve immediately.

Artichokes with Garlic and Parsley

When artichokes are in season, I use them at every opportunity and in many different guises.

A well-known artichoke lover was 14-year-old Catherine de Medici, who moved from her native Tuscany to France as the bride of Henry II. Courtiers were scandalized by her inordinate fondness of artichokes, because these were considered to be an aphrodisiac. Nice women were not supposed to enjoy such food, and certainly not in public.

MAKES 4 SIDE-DISH SERVINGS

6 large artichokes

4 tablespoons extra-virgin olive oil

6 cloves garlic, finely chopped

4 tablespoons chopped parsley

Salt and black pepper

1/2 cup (120ml) water

Snap off artichoke leaves until you come to pale green leaves, with only a little purple showing at the top. Cut off top 2 inches (5cm); leave about 2 inches (5cm) of stalk and cut off the rest.

Trim off any dark green at the bottom and the tough skin of the stalk with a sharp knife or vegetable peeler, until you're left with white flesh around the bottom. Cut artichoke in half lengthwise; remove choke with a teaspoon. Cut halves into quarters and place in a bowl of water acidulated with lemon juice.

Combine oil, garlic and 3 tablespoons of parsley in a sauté pan. Cook over low heat until the garlic is aromatic, but not colored, about 3 minutes. Drain artichokes and toss in oil for a few minutes. Season to taste with salt and pepper. Add water, bring to a simmer and cover pan. Cook over low heat until artichokes are tender, 20 to 25 minutes. If there's too much liquid, uncover the pan, and boil over high heat to reduce. Serve immediately with pan juices, sprinkled with remaining parsley.

Potato, Artichoke and Thyme Gratin

This is one of my cherished winter evening dishes, featuring two of my all-time favorite vegetables.

Both the potatoes and artichokes are fully cooked before they're layered in the dish, and there's a lively interplay of meltingly soft vegetables under a crisp golden top. Serve on its own, or to accompany a meat dish, especially veal.

MAKES 4 SIDE-DISH OR LIGHT MAIN-COURSE SERVINGS

6 large artichokes

4 tablespoons extra-virgin olive oil

6 cloves garlic, finely chopped

3 tablespoons chopped parsley

Salt and black pepper

1/2 cup (120ml) water

4 to 5 very large waxy potatoes

1 tablespoon fresh thyme leaves

6 tablespoons fresh breadcrumbs

Preheat oven to 375F (190C).

Using the first 6 ingredients, follow the method on page 00 for preparing and cooking artichokes, but cut them into 1/3-inch (1cm) thick slices.

Meanwhile, cook potatoes in their skins until tender. Drain, peel, and cut into thick slices, making sure you have enough slices to make two separate layers in your gratin dish. Brush the dish with a little oil and layer with half the potato slices.

Season with salt and pepper. Spoon artichokes and cooking juices over potatoes, sprinkle with thyme, cover with another layer of potatoes. Season with salt and pepper, sprinkle with breadcrumbs and drizzle with remaining oil. Pour about 3 tablespoons water down the sides into the dish and cover with foil. Bake 30 minutes, remove foil and bake 10 minutes more, or until the top is golden and crunchy.

Potato, Garlic and Oregano Gratin with Tomato and Parmesan Topping

Superb when served with grilled chicken, meat or fish, but I am just as happy to eat it all by itself, with a green salad. Don't be misled by the humble ingredients; with good, waxy potatoes and luscious, ripe tomatoes, this indeed is a dish to set before a king.

MAKES 4 SIDE-DISH SERVINGS

2 tablespoons extra-virgin olive oil

1 lb. (500g) waxy potatoes, cut into
   1/8-inch (0.3cm) slices

Salt

2 large cloves garlic, finely
   chopped

1 tablespoon chopped fresh
   oregano

1 lb. (500g) tomatoes, chopped

1 oz./30g (1/3 cup) freshly grated
   Parmesan cheese

1/2 cup (120ml) water

Preheat oven to 375F (190C).

Use 1 tablespoon oil to coat a large gratin dish that will hold the potato slices in one layer, without too much overlapping. Place the potatoes in the dish, season to taste with salt and sprinkle with garlic and oregano. Top with tomatoes and any juices, and the remaining 1 tablespoon oil. Season with salt and sprinkle the cheese over the top. Pour the water into the side of the dish and cover with foil.

Bake 45 minutes or until potatoes are tender when tested. Remove foil and return to the oven for 15 minutes more, or until the cheese is golden, the water has evaporated and the potatoes are crisp on the edges. Serve immediately.

Bread, Tomato and Cucumber Salad
(Fattoush)

Fattoush is the Middle Eastern equivalent of panzanella, *the Italian bread salad, and the different type of bread aside, there's another important ingredient that makes this salad unique: pungent, lemony sumac. Sumac is the crushed red berry of a tree and is used to add lemon flavor without adding extra liquid. Sumac colors everything a shade of pink, red or magenta, depending on the amount used.*

Buy sumac in Middle Eastern food stores. Store sumac in an airtight container in the freezer. If sumac is not available, just use extra lemon juice.

MAKES 4 SIDE-DISH SERVINGS

Dressing

2 large cloves garlic

1/2 teaspoon salt

3 tablespoons lemon juice

2 teaspoons sumac, plus extra for sprinkling

1/4 cup (60ml) extra-virgin olive oil

Black pepper

2 tomatoes, peeled, seeded and cut into 1/3-inch (1cm) cubes

2 cucumbers, peeled, seeded and cubed

1 bunch green onions, thinly sliced

6 tablespoons chopped fresh parsley

2 tablespoons chopped fresh mint leaves

1 bunch arugula, rinsed, spun dry and torn into pieces

1 Turkish *pide* loaf or 2 large pitas

To make the dressing: Combine the garlic and salt in a mortar and crush to a paste. Transfer to a bowl; combine with the lemon juice and sumac. Add the oil in a steady trickle, whisking constantly. Season with extra salt and pepper if necessary. Set aside.

Combine the tomatoes, cucumbers, green onions, parsley, mint and arugula in a large salad bowl and toss with the dressing. Cover with plastic wrap and refrigerate at least 2 hours.

Thirty minutes before serving, slightly wet the bread on both sides and grill under a hot broiler until crisp on both sides, turning once. Tear into bite-sized pieces, cool slightly and toss with the salad. Let stand 10 minutes before serving, with a bowl of extra sumac on the table for sprinkling.

Olives

The Ancient

The whole Mediterranean, the sculpture, the palms, the gold beads, the bearded heroes, the wine, the ideas, the ships, the moonlight, the winged gorgons, the bronze men, the philosopher—all of it seems to me to rise in the sour, pungent taste of these black olives between the teeth. A taste older than meat, older than wine. A taste as old as cold water.

—Lawrence Durrell, *Prospero's Cell*

It's believed that olives were first cultivated in Asia Minor 6,000 years ago and that they spread to Greece from Syria, then to the entire Mediterranean. However, prehistoric fossils and fragments suggest that olive trees existed much earlier than that, as long ago as 12,000 years. There are countless references to olives in ancient cultures: amphoras, frescoes and sarcophagi from the Mycenean culture; Egyptian mummies wearing garlands of woven olive branches; cave paintings from the central Sahara. The Bible makes 140 references to olive oil and close to 100 to the olive tree.

Today's enthusiasm for the olive (*Olea europaea*) and endorsements for its nutritional benefits are nothing new; this is no fleeting passion. And the discovery of the joy of olives and olive oil in countless kitchens around the world is something Mediterranean cooks have been telling us all along.

There are many different types of olives available—I think the most enjoyable way to explore the possibilities is to go to a shop where you can taste before you buy. I have my own mental map of favorite Italian, Greek and Middle Eastern food stores that I visit frequently, and it always feels more like an adventure than a shopping trip. Types of olives include exotic varieties such as niçoise, gaeta and liguria, but for cooking purposes I find that widely available kalamata olives usually have the best flavor and texture, and I recommend you use them in most of the following recipes.

Green olives, because they're picked before fully ripe, tend to be firmer in texture than black ones. There are gadgets available to pit olives, but I find in the case of kalamatas that gentle pressure with the flat blade of a chef's knife opens the olive and the pit is easy to remove. With green olives, it's easier to cut the flesh off the pit with a small knife.

With their robust taste, olives are perfectly suited to combine with bread; all legumes, but especially chickpeas; pasta and polenta; cheese, particularly goat cheese and feta; and strong flavors such as capers, garlic, lemon and chiles. And of course, any combination of olives and tomatoes is Mediterranean cuisine personified.

There's an old story from Greek mythology that I've always liked. According to legend, when Athens was founded there was bitter rivalry between Pallas Athena and Poseidon to name the town, thus the assembly of the gods decided to give the honor to the one who endowed them with the best invention. Poseidon struck the ground with his trident and produced a fine horse, "beautiful, swift, capable of pulling heavy chariots and winning in combat." Athena's gift was an olive tree, "capable of giving a flame for lighting up the night, of soothing wounds, of being a precious food, both rich in flavor and a source of energy." The people voted the olive tree to be of greater benefit to man, granting Athena sovereignty over the region and the city, which bears her name.

Recipes

Tapenade

Aside from the olives, an essential ingredient in this paste is the caper, the little berry inside the unopened flower bud of the caper tree. Although grown in many hot areas, in particular the Sahara, many connoisseurs consider the best capers in the world to be those grown in the south of France. These are gathered by hand when tiny, explaining their high cost. The Provençal word for this berry is tapeno, *hence* tapenade.

This versatile paste may be served on crusty slices of bread, with crudités or with hard-cooked eggs. Try thinning it with pasta cooking water to use as an instant pasta sauce, spread a little on pizza, or dollop on grilled fish. Made in minutes, the sauce keeps in the refrigerator 5 days, but in my house it usually doesn't last that long. Traditionally made in a mortar with pestle, and by purists deemed the only way, I find the food processor does a good job, but make sure not to over-process; the paste should definitely not be smooth.

MAKES ABOUT 1 CUP (230ML)

2 cloves garlic, peeled

1 oz. (30g) flat anchovy fillets, drained

8 oz. (240g) black olives, pitted

2 tablespoons capers, drained

1 tablespoon mixed fresh rosemary and fresh oregano

3 tablespoons extra-virgin olive oil, plus extra

Lemon juice (optional)

Salt and black pepper

Combine garlic, anchovies, olives, capers, herbs and the 3 tablespoons oil in a food processor and process until chopped, although not too finely. Stir in lemon juice, using. Season to taste with salt and pepper, and transfer to a bowl or covered container. Float a little oil on top. Refrigerate until needed. When ready to use, stir the oil into the tapenade and taste for seasoning.

Marinated Olives

Wonderful olives are available to those who take the trouble to find them. Italian, Greek and Middle Eastern delicatessens often have big vats of all manner of olives, which you can try before you buy. I regularly buy olives, as well as beautiful extra-virgin olive oil in large cans, at a fantastic Lebanese food store, where sumac, za'atar, dried lemons, pomegranate molasses and Turkish pide loaves vie for pride of place.

The following quick-and-easy marinade gives olives just that little bit of extra zing.

MAKES 4 SERVINGS

8 oz. (240g) kalamata olives

1/2 teaspoon cumin seeds

1/2 teaspoon fennel seeds

4 sprigs fresh oregano

4 sprigs fresh thyme

1/2 teaspoon fresh rosemary leaves

4 dried hot red chiles

4 cloves garlic, chopped

1/4 cup (120ml) red wine vinegar

Place the olives in a jar that is just the right size to hold them all, with a secure lid. Add all the other ingredients, seal the jar securely and shake well. Top up with water to cover, if necessary. Marinate in the refrigerator for 1 week before using.

Fava Bean Purée
with Olives

Bean purées can be found all along the Mediterranean with slight variations. The Italians purée their cannellini or fava beans and serve them on bruschetta or crostini, the Greeks have their fava—the name of a dish rather than the beans—which are different from Italian fava beans, something like a small version of yellow split peas. There are no hard-and-fast rules about making these bean purées—the following version is quick and easy, and a delight to eat almost any time of the day. I use skinned, split fava beans (the Egyptian ful bean, available at Middle Eastern delis), but any dried beans will do, provided they're properly cooked.

MAKES ABOUT 2 CUPS (460ML)

8 oz. (360g) dried fava beans

1 to 2 fresh hot red chiles, chopped

2 cloves garlic, roughly chopped

2 tablespoons extra-virgin olive oil

Juice of 1/2 lemon or more to taste

Salt and black pepper

12 oz. (360g) kalamata olives

Turkish *pide* or pita bread, to serve

Drain the soaked beans, rinse well and place in a saucepan with water to cover (no salt). Bring to a boil and cook until beans are tender, 30 to 60 minutes. Drain in a colander over a bowl, reserving cooking liquid, and stand 15 minutes to remove excess liquid. Transfer to a food processor or blender while still warm and add chiles, garlic, oil and lemon juice. Process until smooth. Season to taste with salt and pepper. Add a little cooking liquid if the mixture is too dry. Place in a bowl and refrigerate a few hours or overnight. Serve on a large platter and surround with olives and torn pieces of bread.

Olive, Lemon
and Chile Sauce

A North African sauce, which transforms a plain grilled or pan-fried piece of fish, meat or chicken into something wonderful and exotic; you can also use it for a quick, no-cook pasta sauce. Both black and green olives are used, which gives the sauce a more interesting flavor and texture, although naturally it may be made with just one kind.

MAKES ABOUT 1/2 CUP (120ML)

2 teaspoons cumin seeds

3 tablespoons lemon juice

6 cloves garlic, finely chopped

2 teaspoons mild paprika

2 fresh hot red chiles, chopped
(seeds removed, if desired)

2 tablespoons extra-virgin olive oil

3 tablespoons chopped fresh
cilantro leaves

1/2 lemon, finely chopped, both
the zest and the flesh

8 each large black and green olives,
pitted and coarsely chopped

Place cumin seeds in a small dry frying pan over medium heat until aromatic, shaking the pan frequently, about 3 minutes. Pulverize in a mortar and combine in a bowl with the lemon juice, garlic, paprika and chiles.

Add oil, cilantro, lemon zest and flesh, and olives. Stir vigorously until well amalgamated. Store in the refrigerator in a covered jar up to 2 weeks.

Olive and Rosemary Focaccia

When cut into small squares, this focaccia makes a great nibble to serve with drinks. Sometimes I make half-quantities of both the Olive and Rosemary and the Garlic and Parmesan Focaccia. It makes good picnic fare, too.

MAKES 2 (8-INCH/20-CM) FOCACCE

Focaccia (see Garlic and Parmesan Focaccia, pages 60-61)

Cornmeal

Olive and Rosemary Topping

3 tablespoons extra-virgin olive oil

1 large onion, halved, cut into thin slices

2 large cloves garlic, thinly sliced

1 tablespoon fresh rosemary leaves

Salt and black pepper

12 kalamata olives, pitted and halved

Rosemary sprigs

Make the focaccia according to the directions on page 61.

To make the topping, combine oil and onion in a frying pan and cook onion stirring frequently, 3 minutes. Add garlic and cook, stirring, 1 minute. Add rosemary, season to taste with salt and pepper; cook 1 minute more. Set aside to cool.

Preheat oven, with baking tiles installed, to 425F (220C).

Roll dough, one ball at a time, on a generously floured surface until you have 2 (8-inch/20-cm) circles.

Transfer the focacce to a baking sheet sprinkled with cornmeal. Spread onion-and-rosemary mixture on top of focacce, leaving a 3/4-inch (2-cm) border. With floured fingers, make indentations all over the surface. Place in a draft-free place to rise, 45 to 60 minutes. Transfer to a peel or upside-down baking sheet sprinkled with cornmeal, arrange olives on top and sprinkle with extra rosemary sprigs. Sprinkle baking tiles with cornmeal and slide focacce into the oven. Bake 30 minutes, or until golden. Serve immediately.

Cannellini Bean Soup with Bell Peppers and Olives

With its little yellow- and red- bell pepper squares, marinated in vinegar, and small black olive strips, this Greek bean soup has to be one of the prettiest I've ever seen. Vinegar gives the sweet pepper added flavor. I suggest serving this soup at room temperature, rather than warm or hot.

MAKES 4 FIRST-COURSE SERVINGS

1 red bell pepper, halved, seeded

1 yellow bell pepper, halved, seeded

1 carrot, scraped

1 stalk celery

2 tablespoons extra-virgin olive oil

2 tablespoons red-wine vinegar

Salt and black pepper

1 red onion, chopped

2 cloves garlic, finely chopped

8 oz. (240g) cannellini beans, soaked

4 cups (1 liter) water

6 kalamata olives, pitted, slivered

Cut bell peppers, carrot and celery into pea-sized cubes, keeping the ingredients separate. Combine 1 tablespoon oil in a pan with bell peppers, cover tightly and cook until soft, stirring occasionally, 10 to 15 minutes. Remove from heat, stir in vinegar and season to taste with salt and pepper. Set aside.

Combine remaining oil in another pan with carrot, celery and onion, and cook until soft, stirring frequently, 5 to 7 minutes. Add garlic and stir 1 minute more.

Drain beans and add them to the pan with the water. Bring to the boil, stirring frequently, then reduce heat to low, cover pan and simmer over low heat until beans are tender, about 1-1/2 hours.

Stir in bell peppers, and serve warm or at room temperature, sprinkled with the olives.

Ricotta Tart with Basil and Olives

This pretty, green-flecked tart makes an ideal summer lunch or supper, or thin wedges could be used as part of an antipasto platter. Always serve at room temperature. If you're in a hurry, use frozen pastry.

Short Crust pastry

4 oz./120g (1/2 cup) unsalted butter, cubed and frozen for 15 minutes

1-3/4 cups (425g) all-purpose flour

Pinch of salt

1 egg yolk

Iced water

1/2 cup (120ml) extra-virgin olive oil

1 small onion, finely chopped

1 clove garlic, finely chopped

3/4 cup (175ml) fresh basil leaves

1/3 cup (175ml) fresh parsley leaves

Salt and black pepper

1 lb. (500g) fresh ricotta cheese

1 large egg and 1 yolk, whisked together

1 oz./130g (1/3 cup) freshly grated Parmesan cheese

12 kalamata olives, pitted, chopped

To make the pastry: Combine butter, flour and salt in a food processor and pulse until the mixture resembles coarse breadcrumbs. Add egg yolk and, with motor running, enough iced water until the mixture holds together.

Remove to a floured surface, knead into a ball and flatten. Cover with plastic wrap and refrigerate 30 minutes. Remove the dough from the refrigerator and roll it out to fit into a 9-inch (23-cm) loose-bottomed, fluted tart pan and prick the bottom all over with a fork. Line with foil, following the contours of the pastry, and refrigerate or freeze 30 minutes.

Preheat oven to 375F (190C). Fill foil-lined pastry shell with baking weights, dried peas, beans or rice, and bake blind 10 minutes. Remove weights and foil carefully and bake 10 minutes more, or until the pastry is set. Remove from oven and set aside until cool. Reduce oven temperature to 350F (180C).

Combine oil and onion in a frying pan and cook over medium heat until onion is soft, about 5 minutes. Add garlic and cook 1 minute more. Remove from heat and cool.

Combine basil and parsley in a food processor with the cooled oil mixture and process until finely chopped. Season to taste with salt and pepper. Place ricotta in a large bowl and gently fold in egg mixture, then Parmesan cheese. Fold in basil mixture and olives. Spoon into cooled pastry shell and bake 30 minutes, or until just set. Serve warm.

Pasta with Olive, Walnut and Basil Sauce

An uncooked pasta sauce with a few of the elements of puttanesca, but it omits tomatoes and includes walnuts. With a few herbs from your own garden and pantry standbys, you can put together this fragrant sauce in no time at all. It's also great on boiled potatoes, making a potato salad with a difference, or grilled fish.

The fragrance develops instantly when the cool sauce is combined with the hot ingredients, a true flavor explosion.

MAKES 6 FIRST-COURSE OR
4 MAIN-COURSE SERVINGS

1/4 cup (60ml) chopped walnuts

1 cup (230ml) fresh basil leaves, coarsely chopped

1/2 cup (120ml) fresh flat-leaf parsley leaves, coarsely chopped

12 kalamata olives, pitted and coarsely chopped

2 oz./60g (2/3 cup) freshly grated Parmesan cheese

4 anchovy fillets, rinsed, chopped

2 fresh hot red chiles, finely sliced (seeds removed, if desired)

2 cloves garlic, finely chopped

2 teaspoons capers, drained, chopped

1/2 cup (120ml) extra-virgin olive oil

1 lb. (500g) dried pasta, such as linguine or fusilli

Preheat oven to 350F (180C).

Spread walnuts on a baking sheet and toast in the oven about 10 minutes. Set aside to cool.

Combine basil, parsley, olives, Parmesan cheese, anchovies, chiles, garlic, capers and toasted walnuts in a pasta bowl and mix well. Add oil and stir to combine.

Meanwhile, cook the pasta in boiling, salted water until al dente, then drain. Transfer to the bowl containing the olive mixture and toss to combine. Serve immediately.

Pasta with Marinated Seafood, Tomatoes, Olives and Basil

When preparing this dish, I have no trouble imagining myself in a centuries-old kitchen with plastered walls and windows with flimsy curtains billowing softly in the Mediterranean breeze. A large bowl of lemons sits on a wooden table—which is my kitchen workbench as well as the place where we eat—and the sun is shining.

MAKES 6 FIRST-COURSE OR
4 MAIN-COURSE SERVINGS

2 lb. (1kg) black mussels

2 teaspoons plus 1/4 cup (60ml)
    extra-virgin olive oil

8 oz. (240g) calamari (squid) rings

1 lb. (500g) medium raw shrimp,
    peeled and deveined

1 clove garlic, finely chopped

2 tomatoes, peeled,
    each cut into 8 to 12 wedges

16 kalamata olives, pitted, halved

6 tablespoons lemon juice

1/2 cup (60ml) fresh basil leaves,
    torn into bite-sized pieces

Salt and black pepper

1 lb. (500g) short pasta shapes

Soak the mussels in a sink or bowl of salted water 1 hour. Scrub if necessary and pull away the beards. Transfer to a pan, with water adhering, cover; place over high heat, shaking pan frequently, until mussels have opened, about 5 minutes. Discard mussels that won't open. Remove mussels from shells and place in a bowl.

Heat 2 teaspoons oil in a small frying pan, add calamari and shrimp, and cook until opaque, turning once, about 3 minutes. Add to bowl.

Add garlic, tomatoes, olives, 1/4 cup (60ml) oil, lemon juice and basil to bowl. Season to taste with salt and pepper. Cover with plastic wrap; set aside to marinate 30 minutes at room temperature or, in the refrigerator, up to 1 hour.

Cook pasta in boiling, salted water until al dente, drain and add to seafood. Toss well and serve.

Pasta with Belgian Endive, Tomatoes, Olives and Pancetta

This pasta came about by way of experimenting with Belgian endive, one of my favorite pasta-sauce ingredients. It's not common in pasta sauces, but it seems to possess the right characteristics. When slicing the Belgian endive, don't stop at the white core; its inclusion gives the sauce texture and definition.

MAKES 6 FIRST-COURSE OR 4 MAIN-COURSE SERVINGS

3 tablespoons extra-virgin olive oil

2 oz. (60g) thinly sliced pancetta, cut into strips

4 cloves garlic, chopped

1/2 teaspoon hot chile flakes

4 large tomatoes, finely chopped

Salt and black pepper

12 kalamata olives, pitted, chopped

4 large heads Belgian endive, very thinly sliced crosswise

1 lb. (500g) pasta, such as fettuccine or bavette

Combine oil and pancetta in a frying pan and cook over medium heat until the pancetta is crisp, about 5 minutes. Remove with a slotted spoon, drain on paper towels and set aside. Add garlic and chile flakes to the pan and cook 1 minute more. Add tomatoes, season to taste with salt and pepper, and cook over medium-low heat until the sauce is slightly thickened, 12 to 15 minutes.

Stir in the olives and keep warm. Place the Belgian endive in a shallow bowl.

Meanwhile, cook the pasta in boiling, salted water until al dente, then drain. Pour tomato sauce over the Belgian endive and immediately top with hot pasta. Toss well and serve, sprinkled with pancetta.

Al Forno Pasta with Cheese, Tomato and Olives

Al forno *means "in the oven," thus all Italian dishes that are baked, such as lasagne, are* al forno, *but the term is not restricted to pasta. This particular pasta is so appealing because the flavors are strong and gutsy, with a modest spark of chile within and a little garlic baked right on top.*

MAKES 6 MAIN-COURSE SERVINGS

2 tablespoons extra-virgin olive oil

1 large red onion, chopped

3 cloves garlic, finely chopped

2 lb. (1kg) tomatoes, peeled, seeded, chopped

1/2 to 1 teaspoon hot chile flakes

Salt and black pepper

1/2 cup (120ml) fresh basil leaves, torn into pieces

1 lb. (500g) penne pasta

8 oz. (240g) grated Gruyère

2-1/2 oz. (75g) kalamata olives, pitted and halved

1/2 cup (45g) grated Parmesan cheese, for topping

Preheat oven to 375F (190C). Lightly oil a 3-quart (3-liter) baking dish.

Combine oil and onion in a Dutch oven and cook, stirring frequently, until soft, about 5 minutes. Add 2 of chopped garlic cloves and stir 1 minute, until aromatic. Add tomatoes and chile flakes, and cook until tomatoes soften, but still hold their shape, 5 to 8 minutes. Season with salt and pepper, and stir in basil.

Meanwhile, cook the pasta in boiling, salted water until nearly al dente, then drain. Transfer to a large bowl, add the grated cheese and stir until it melts.

Gently fold in tomato mixture, check seasoning and transfer to the baking dish. Dot with the olives and sprinkle with Parmesan and remaining garlic. Bake about 30 minutes, or until bubbling and golden.

Polenta Gratin with Fennel, Tomato, Pancetta and Olives

A great treat for hearty winter appetites, the delicate fennel taste is enhanced by the robust flavors of pancetta, tomatoes and olives. I use firm tomatoes that won't disintegrate during cooking.

Make the polenta well ahead of time, because it needs a few hours to cool to room temperature. You'll have more than you'll need for this dish; wrap securely what remains and refrigerate or freeze for future use.

MAKES 4 MAIN-COURSE SERVINGS

Polenta

7-3/4 cups (1.9 liter) water

3 tablespoons extra-virgin olive oil

3 teaspoons salt

12 oz. (360g) polenta

Fennel, Tomato, Pancetta and Olives

1 fennel bulb (about 1-1/2 lb./750g), trimmed

4 cloves garlic, finely chopped

2 tablespoons extra-virgin olive oil

2 oz. (60g) pancetta, cut into strips

1/2 cup (100ml) water

Salt and black pepper

4 large plum tomatoes, peeled, seeded and cut into pieces

2 teaspoons chopped fresh oregano

12 kalamata olives, pitted, chopped

3/4 cup (120g) grated Gruyère cheese

1/3 cup (130g) grated Parmesan cheese

To make the polenta, bring water to a boil in a large saucepan, add oil and salt and, when boiling again, pour in polenta in a steady stream, stirring constantly. Cook over low heat, stirring constantly, until polenta pulls away from the sides of the pan, about 20 minutes. Pour into lightly oiled cake pans and set aside to cool.

Preheat oven to 375F (190C). Cut fennel in half

through the core, then into quarters. Cut the quarters into 3 wedges each, making sure the core stays attached to each wedge. Combine the fennel, garlic and oil in a Dutch oven and cook over medium-low heat, stirring frequently, 3 minutes. Add the pancetta and cook 5 minutes more, stirring frequently. Add the water and season to taste with salt and pepper. Bring to a simmer, cover and cook very gently 30 minutes, or until the cores are tender when tested. Add the tomatoes, oregano and olives, increase heat to medium and cook until the water has evaporated, about 5 minutes. Check seasoning and transfer to a shallow baking dish.

Cut the polenta into 1/3-inch (1-cm) slices and arrange over the vegetables, slightly overlapping. Sprinkle with the combined cheeses, cover with foil and bake 30 minutes. Remove the foil and bake 20 minutes more, or until the top is golden and the filling is bubbling. Let stand a few minutes before serving on heated plates.

Risotto with Prosciutto, Lemon and Olives

Lemon zest and juice contribute lightness and zip to this risotto, while the prosciutto and olives provide distinct flavors. Don't add too much salt during cooking, because these ingredients are salty enough by themselves.

MAKES 4 MAIN-COURSE SERVINGS

3 tablespoons extra-virgin olive oil

1 onion, finely chopped

4 oz.(120g) sliced prosciutto: 2 oz. (60g) chopped and 2 oz. (60g) cut into strips

2 teaspoons grated lemon zest

2 cloves garlic, finely chopped

2 cups (400g) arborio rice

1/2 cup (120ml) dry white wine

6 cups (1.4 liters) chicken stock, simmering

Salt and black pepper

16 kalamata olives, pitted, chopped

2/3 cup (60g) freshly grated Parmesan cheese

2 tablespoons lemon juice

Combine oil and onion in a heavy saucepan and cook stirring frequently, until onion is soft, about 5 minutes. Add chopped prosciutto, lemon zest and garlic, and cook, stirring, 1 minute.

Add rice and stir a few minutes to coat the grains, then add wine. Stir until the wine has been absorbed, then start adding simmering stock by the ladleful. Keep adding a ladleful of stock when the previous one has been absorbed, 20 to 25 minutes. Season lightly about halfway through the cooking time, keeping in mind the saltiness of the prosciutto, olives and cheese. If the stock runs out, add simmering water. Reserve a few tablespoons of stock to add last.

Add reserved stock, strips of prosciutto, olives, Parmesan cheese and lemon juice. Stir vigorously 1 minute, cover pan and remove from heat. Let stand 3 minutes before serving.

Risotto with Sausage, Red Wine and Olives

Not for people who are shy about eating, this risotto is a filling, robust meal, although surprisingly light and lively in flavor. You'll find the Italian fennel-scented sausage meat doesn't break up into small bits, so there are smallish chunks of meat in the rosy-hued mass of creamy rice, accented with the olives.

MAKES 4 MAIN-COURSE SERVINGS

3 tablespoons extra-virgin olive oil

1 large red onion, chopped

1 lb. (500g) bulk Italian sausage

2 cups (400g) arborio rice

1 cup (230ml) robust red wine

6 cups (1.4 liters) chicken stock, simmering

Salt and black pepper

12 kalamata olives, pitted, chopped

2/3 cup (60g) freshly grated Parmesan cheese

1/4 cup (60ml) chopped parsley

Combine oil and onion in a heavy saucepan, and cook over medium heat until soft, stirring frequently, about 5 minutes. Add sausage and cook 5 minutes more, stirring frequently. Add rice and stir 2 minutes, until all the rice is coated with oil. Add wine and stir until absorbed, about 2 minutes. Start adding simmering stock one ladleful at a time, adding another ladleful when the previous one has been absorbed. Cook 20 to 25 minutes. Season lightly with salt and pepper about halfway through the cooking time, bearing in mind the saltiness of the olives and cheese. If the stock runs out, add simmering water. Reserve a few tablespoons of the stock to add last.

Add reserved stock, olives, cheese and parsley, and stir vigorously. Cover saucepan and let stand 3 minutes before serving.

Chicory with Cannellini Beans, Garlic and Olives

One of a range of fabulous bean dishes found all around the Mediterranean. Substitute fava beans for the Italian cannellini bean and we're in the Middle East, switch to chickpeas, add a few spices, such as cumin and fresh cilantro, and we're in North Africa. Egyptian fava beans, also known as ful medames, *are smaller than regular fava beans, with a distinctive flavor and mealy texture. They are available at Middle Eastern food stores or health food stores.*

MAKES 3 OR 4 MAIN-COURSE SERVINGS

1 15-oz. (425g) can cannellini beans

2 tablespoons extra-virgin olive oil

4 cloves garlic, finely chopped

1/4 teaspoon hot chile flakes

1 bunch chicory or Swiss chard, bottom stems discarded, rinsed, cut into strips

Salt and black pepper

2 plum tomatoes, halved, seeded and chopped

8 kalamata olives, pitted, chopped

Lemon wedges and crusty bread, to serve

Place beans in a saucepan with plenty of water to cover (no salt) and bring slowly to a boil. Simmer gently 10 minutes. Drain and reserve the cooking liquid.

Meanwhile, combine oil, garlic and chile flakes in a Dutch oven. Cook over medium-low heat, stirring frequently, until aromatic, 2 to 3 minutes. Add chicory and cook until wilted, about 3 minutes. Add drained beans and enough cooking liquid to come halfway up the sides of the vegetables. Season to taste with salt and pepper, and simmer gently 10 minutes. Stir in tomatoes and olives, and simmer 5 minutes, or until heated through. Serve immediately.

Lentils with Potato, Lemon, Arugula and Olives

Use green or brown lentils in this recipe, not the red ones that cook into a mush. The French lentilles vertes du Puy are also excellent but are more expensive.

MAKES 4 MAIN-COURSE SERVINGS

3 tablespoons extra-virgin olive oil

4 large cloves garlic, chopped

1/2 teaspoon hot chile flakes

2 cups (460ml) brown or green
   lentils, picked over and rinsed

6 cups (1.4 liters) water

1-1/2 lb. (750g) potatoes, cubed

2 large or 4 small bunches arugula

1/4 cup (60ml) lemon juice

16 kalamata olives, pitted, halved

Salt and black pepper

Lemon wedges and Italian bread

Combine the oil, garlic and chile flakes in a Dutch oven and cook, stirring frequently, over very low heat 10 minutes, without coloring the garlic. Add lentils and stir a few minutes to coat with oil. Add the water and bring to a simmer. Cover and simmer 10 minutes. Add potatoes and cook, uncovered, 20 minutes, or until lentils and potatoes are tender. Add more water if necessary.

Stir in arugula, lemon juice and olives, cover and cook 5 minutes, or until arugula has wilted. Season to taste with salt and pepper, and serve in heated, deep plates with lemon wedges and Italian bread.

Tomato, Olive and Feta Tabbouleh

There tends to be some confusion about bulgur, which is used to make tabbouleh, and cracked wheat. The spelling alone is confusing: you'll find bulgur, bulgar, burghul *or* bourghul, *depending on the country of origin. Paula Wolfert, the eminent Middle Eastern food writer, says* bulgur, *so I'll use that. Bulgur is wheat, cooked and parched before grinding, and it only needs to soak in liquid to become fully digestible.*

Bulgur is available coarsely and finely ground. For salads, the coarse ground is recommended, whereas the fine ground is suitable for making kibbeh, *a Middle Eastern meatball. Cracked wheat is uncooked wheat berries broken into fragments, but is wrongly referred to as bulgur.*

MAKE 6 SIDE-DISH SERVINGS

1 lb. (500g) coarse bulgur

2 tablespoons extra-virgin olive oil, plus extra for serving

3 tablespoons lemon juice

Salt and black pepper

4 green onions, finely sliced

1 lb. (500g) tomatoes, chopped

8 oz. (240g) feta cheese

4 oz. (120g) kalamata olives, pitted

1/4 cup (60ml) torn fresh basil leaves

Place bulgur in a 4-cup measuring cup and add the same amount of water. Set aside 1 hour. Drain if necessary. Fluff with a fork and transfer to a large bowl. Stir in oil and lemon juice, and season to taste with salt and pepper, adding more lemon juice if desired.

Add green onions, tomatoes, feta cheese, olives and basil, and toss gently. Serve cold, with extra olive oil.

Fish Fillets Baked on Potatoes, with Garlic and Olives

Buy thick, white, firm-fleshed fillets for this scrumptious main course, the perfect one-dish meal; I usually choose halibut, snapper or sea bass. The potatoes are baked first until tender, then the fish is cooked on top, the potatoes become crisp, and the whole dish is enveloped in a mellow garlic aroma.

MAKES 4 MAIN-COURSE SERVINGS

2 large cloves garlic, finely
   chopped

6 tablespoons chopped parsley

3 tablespoons extra-virgin olive oil

1-1/4 lb.(750g) waxy potatoes,
   peeled and thinly sliced

Salt and black pepper

4 thick, white, fish fillets

12 kalamata olives, pitted, halved

Preheat oven to 400F (200C). Lightly grease a gratin or baking dish.

Combine garlic, parsley and oil and divide the mixture in half. Combine one half with the potatoes and season to taste with salt and pepper. Toss well and layer in the gratin or baking dish. Bake 15 minutes, or until the potatoes are almost tender.

Place the fish on top in a single layer, skin-side down. Brush with remaining garlic, parsley and oil mixture and season to taste with salt and pepper. Bake 15 to 20 minutes, or until the fish is cooked through and the potatoes are crisp. Add the olives the last 5 minutes of cooking. Serve immediately.

Baked Tuna in *Chermoula*, with Tomatoes and Olives

Chermoula is a Moroccan mixture of herbs and spices, used with great effect to enhance the natural flavors of fish, chicken and meat. First the mixture, which almost always contains a mixture of pungent spices, is assembled, then rubbed into the food and left to marinate several hours or overnight. If you like even more of a flavor explosion, add some slivered preserved lemon to the tomato and olive mixture. The charm of this dish lies in the subtle yet vibrant flavors of the tuna baking in the herbs and spices, under its blanket of fresh tomato and olives. Any other thick fish fillets work well here; try snapper, sea bass, swordfish or halibut.

Serve with couscous, roasted potatoes or crusty bread.

MAKES 4 MAIN-COURSE SERVINGS

4 tuna steaks, 1 inch (2.5cm) thick

Chermoula

1/4 teaspoon cumin seeds

1 small red onion, finely chopped

2 cloves garlic, chopped

1/8 teaspoon mild paprika

1 hot red chile, minced

2 tablespoons chopped fresh cilantro leaves

2 tablespoons chopped parsley

2 tablespoons extra-virgin olive oil

1 tablespoon lemon juice

Salt

Topping

4 tomatoes, peeled, chopped

2 tablespoons chopped parsley

8 black olives, pitted and halved

Salt and black pepper

To make the *chermoula*: Place the cumin seeds in a small dry frying pan over medium heat. Shake the pan frequently, until the seeds start to color slightly and are aromatic, about 3 minutes. Cool slightly and pulverize in a mortar. Combine the ground cumin in a bowl with the remaining *chermoula* ingredients.

Place tuna steaks in a baking dish in a single layer. Spoon the *chermoula* on top and distribute evenly over the fish. Turn the fish once, so both sides are coated. Cover the dish with plastic wrap and refrigerate at least 2 hours, or overnight. Remove from the refrigerator 30 minutes before cooking to return to room temperature.

Meanwhile, make the topping. Combine the tomatoes, parsley and olives in a bowl, and lightly season with salt and pepper.

Preheat oven to 400F (200C). Spread the tomato mixture over the fish, cover the dish with foil and bake 20 minutes, or until done when tested. Serve immediately on heated plates.

Pan-fried Fish Fillets with Fresh Tomato Sauce

As easy to cook for just one person as for a crowd, this simple recipe is absolutely delicious. The sauce, which is really more like a salsa, has a fresh, uncomplicated quality with plenty of flavor contributed by the olives, capers, sun-dried tomatoes, herbs and lemon juice.

MAKES 4 MAIN-COURSE SERVINGS

2 tablespoons unsalted butter

4 fish fillets, such as halibut

Tomato, Olive and Caper Sauce

4 plum tomatoes, chopped

8 black olives

1 tablespoon capers, drained and chopped

3 tablespoons chopped sun-dried tomatoes in oil, drained

2 tablespoons chopped parsley

2 tablespoons chopped fresh oregano

2 tablespoons extra-virgin olive oil

2 tablespoons lemon juice

Salt and black pepper

To make the sauce: Add all the ingredients to a bowl and toss well. Taste and adjust seasonings if desired. Set aside at room temperature 1 hour, or cover and refrigerate several hours. Remove from refrigerator 30 minutes before serving to return to room temperature.

Melt the butter in a large frying pan over medium heat. Add fish, skin side down (if present), and fry 3 minutes. Turn the fish gently and cook the other side until the fish is cooked through, 2 to 4 minutes more, depending on thickness. Transfer to heated plates, surround with the sauce and serve immediately.

Pork Chops with Green Olives, Rosemary and Lemon

Made in a jiffy, these down-home pork chops are a perfect showcase for pork and rosemary. I have several rosemary shrubs in my garden at all times, because I use this herb in many meat dishes, such as these pork chops, a slowly simmered rolled shoulder of veal, with sautéed shrimp, and to flavor potatoes while roasting.

MAKES 4 MAIN-COURSE SERVINGS

2 tablespoons extra-virgin olive oil

4 thick pork loin chops, bone in and fat removed, if desired

2 cloves garlic, chopped

1 tablespoon fresh rosemary leaves, roughly chopped

3 tablespoons dry white wine

1/4 cup (60ml) water

3 oz. (120g) green olives, pitted and thinly sliced crosswise

Salt and black pepper

Lemon juice to taste

Heat a large cast-iron frying pan over medium-high heat. Add 1 tablespoon oil and, when hot but not smoking, add pork chops and cook until golden brown and cooked through, 10 to 12 minutes, turning once. Remove to a plate; cover to keep warm.

Add remaining oil to the frying pan, then add the garlic and rosemary. Stir over medium heat until aromatic, about 1 minute.

Add the wine and water, bring to a boil, scraping up any browned bits from the bottom of the pan, and cook until the liquid is reduced to 1/4 cup (60ml). Stir in olives, season to taste with salt, pepper and lemon juice. Transfer chops to heated plates and spoon the sauce over the top.

Portuguese Beef Stew with Almonds and Olives

There's an enchanting story that explains the proliferation of almond trees in Portugal. Legend has it that a Portuguese prince married a Swedish princess who became homesick for the winter snowfields of Sweden. To make her feel more at home, the prince planted almond trees along the Portuguese seaboard, so the blossoms would blanket the ground in a white veil in springtime. Surely they lived happily ever after.

MAKES 4 TO 6 MAIN-COURSE SERVINGS

1 oz./30g (1/3 cup) slivered almonds

2 tablespoons extra-virgin olive oil

1-1/2 lb. (750g) stew beef, cubed

2 large onions, chopped

1 tablespoon mild paprika

1/4 teaspoon hot chile flakes

2 cloves garlic, chopped

3/4 cup (175ml) dry red wine

1 cup (230ml) water

Salt and black pepper

1/2 cup (120ml) parsley, chopped

10 to 12 kalamata olives, pitted and roughly chopped

Preheat oven to 350F (180C).

Spread almonds on a baking sheet and toast in the oven 10 minutes, or until golden. Set aside to cool.

Heat a heavy frying pan over high heat, add 1 tablespoon oil and sear the beef cubes in batches, on all sides, about 4 minutes each batch. Remove to a Dutch oven, and repeat the procedure until all the cubes have been seared.

Add remaining oil and the onions to the frying pan and cook over medium heat until the onion is soft, stirring frequently, about 5 minutes. Add paprika, chile flakes and garlic, and cook, stirring, 2 minutes more. Transfer onion mixture to Dutch oven with the beef.

Pour 1/4 cup (60ml) red wine into the frying pan, bring to a boil and cook, stirring, over high heat 1 minute, scraping up any browned bits from the bottom. Pour into the Dutch oven with the remaining wine and enough of the water to barely cover the beef. Season to taste with salt and pepper. Bring to a simmer, cover pan and simmer 1 hour. Stir in the almonds and simmer 30 minutes more, or until beef is tender. Taste for seasoning. Stir in parsley and olives and serve immediately.

Minute Steaks with Tomatoes, Olives and Oregano

Much confusion surrounds the herbs oregano and marjoram, and indeed they are closely related. Fortunately there is not so much difference between them that it could ruin a dish. Oregano has a strong, pungent flavor, whereas marjoram is more demure. Both are easy to grow in pots, and oregano, in particular, can withstand arid conditions in hot, sunny climates, as well as the cold of more temperate zones.

MAKES 4 MAIN-COURSE SERVINGS

2 tablespoons plus 2 teaspoons extra-virgin olive oil

1 onion, thinly sliced

2 cloves garlic, chopped

2 tomatoes, finely chopped

2 teaspoons chopped fresh oregano leaves

Salt and black pepper

12 kalamata olives, pitted and roughly chopped

1 lb. (500g) very thin beef steaks, sides slashed to prevent curling

Combine the 2 tablespoons oil and onion in a sauté pan. Cook over medium heat until the onion is soft, stirring frequently, about 5 minutes. Add the garlic and cook until aromatic, 1 minute. Stir in the tomatoes and oregano, bring to a simmer and cook gently until the sauce slightly thickens, about 15 minutes. Season to taste with salt and pepper and stir in the olives. Keep warm over low heat.

Heat a cast-iron frying pan over high heat, add the remaining oil and, when hot but not smoking, add beef and brown on both sides, 20 to 30 seconds each side. Season with salt, then add the beef to the pan containing the tomato sauce and turn a few times in the sauce to coat. Serve on heated plates, and spoon over the sauce.

Chicken Tagine with Preserved Lemons and Olives

If there's one dish that personifies the wonderful food of Morocco, it has to be this particular tagine, but it tends toward overkill. When I was there last, even the mention of this dish after a few days produced much heavy rolling of eyes in our group of food writers, and by the end of the trip no one imagined, once home, they would be likely to cook it. I overcame my reluctance and came up with this version—simple to make and very, very good.

MAKES 4 MAIN-COURSE SERVINGS

1 (3-lb./1.5kg) chicken, halved

6 tablespoons extra-virgin olive oil

1 tablespoon ground turmeric

Salt and black pepper

1 large onion, thinly sliced

1 tomato, chopped

6 tablespoons chopped parsley

4 large cloves garlic, chopped

3 tablespoons lemon juice

2 preserved lemons, pulp removed, peel cut into thin strips

9-1/2 oz. (280g) black olives, pitted

Couscous or steamed rice

Rub the chicken all over with oil and turmeric, sprinkle with salt and grind over plenty of black pepper. Place in a Dutch oven and add onion, tomato, parsley, garlic and lemon juice. Bring to a simmer, cover and simmer over medium heat until the chicken is tender, about 90 minutes.

Remove chicken from the pan and transfer to a very low oven (250F/120C) to keep warm. Remove as much of the fat on top of the cooking liquid as possible.

Return chicken to the pan, add preserved lemon strips and olives, and simmer 10 minutes. Serve with couscous or rice.

Chicken with Tomato, Feta and Olives

Here's a light, fresh, simple main course, made in one pot. The creamy appearance belies the fact it's low on calories, but high on flavor. I like to serve this with basmati rice; the nutty flavor goes well with the sauce. Crusty bread is a must to mop up the delicious sauce.

MAKES 4 MAIN-COURSE SERVINGS

2 tablespoons extra-virgin olive oil

1-1/4 lb. (650g) boneless chicken thighs, cut into bite-size pieces

Salt and black pepper

1 large onion, chopped

2 to 4 cloves garlic, finely chopped

1/2 cup (120ml) dry white wine

4 tomatoes, peeled, seeded and chopped

1/4 to 1/2 teaspoon hot chile flakes

1 tablespoon plus 1 teaspoon finely chopped fresh oregano

4 oz. (120g) feta cheese, crumbled

12 kalamata olives, pitted, halved

3 tablespoons chopped parsley

Heat the oil in a Dutch oven, add chicken, in batches, and brown on all sides. Remove chicken from the pan, set aside and season lightly with salt and pepper.

Add onion to the pan and cook until soft, stirring frequently, 5 minutes. Add garlic and cook, stirring, 1 minute. Add wine and bring to a boil, scraping up browned bits from the bottom. Add tomatoes, chile flakes and 1 tablespoon oregano.

Season to taste with salt and pepper.

Return chicken to the pan, along with any juices, and simmer uncovered 20 to 30 minutes, or until sauce has thickened and chicken is cooked. Stir in feta cheese and olives, cover pan and cook 5 minutes, or until the cheese has melted into the sauce. Stir in parsley and the remaining 1 teaspoon oregano and serve immediately in deep plates.

Roast Duck with
Red Wine and Olive Sauce

When making this robust but festive meal, you can keep your hands free to do something else in the meantime; it virtually cooks itself. The great Brillat-Savarin has been quoted as saying, in a somewhat understated fashion, that he considered duck "slightly exciting" and that it induced dreaming; furthermore, that certain sauces served with duck were "monstrous, degrading and dishonorable." I wonder what he'd think of the following?

MAKES 4 MAIN-COURSE SERVINGS

1 (about 5-lb./2.2-kg) duck, rinsed inside and out, dried and seasoned with salt

3/4 cup (175ml) red wine

12 black olives, pitted and halved

3 large cloves garlic, chopped

1 teaspoon fresh thyme leaves

2 tablespoons chopped parsley

1 large ripe tomato, finely chopped

Salt and black pepper

1/2 cup (120ml) water

Preheat oven to 400F (200C). Prick the duck all over with a sharp skewer, place on a rack in a roasting pan and roast 45 minutes.

Meanwhile, combine the wine, olives, garlic, thyme, parsley and tomato in a bowl and season with salt and pepper. Stir in the water and set aside.

After 45 minutes, pour off fat from roasting pan; add wine and olive mixture. Decrease oven heat to 325F (160C) and roast 45 minutes

more, or until juices run clear when the thigh is pierced.

Remove duck to a cutting board and keep warm. Remove rack from pan, place pan over high heat and stir until sauce has slightly thickened. Pour into a heated bowl. Carve the duck and place on a heated platter. Serve immediately with sauce.

Bean and Fish Salad
with Cucumber and Olives

I love to serve this stunning salad on sultry summer evenings. Although it can be made with any type of fish or shellfish, such as shrimp, I prefer to use sea trout or salmon. It's a perfect excuse to poach a whole fish. For a colorful change, use yellow pear tomatoes—or half red, half yellow.

MAKES 8 MAIN-COURSE SERVINGS

12 oz. (360g) cannellini beans, soaked

3 tablespoons extra-virgin olive oil

Salt

2 lb. (1kg) cooked, firm fish, broken into bite-size pieces

1 cucumber, peeled and sliced

1 lb. (500g) cherry tomatoes, halved

24 kalamata olives, pitted and halved

1/2 cup (120ml) torn fresh basil leaves

Assorted greens, such as mesclun, watercress, arugula or radicchio

6 tablespoons lemon juice

Drain and rinse the soaked beans, place in a saucepan with water to cover (no salt) and bring slowly to a boil. Simmer until beans are tender, 40 to 60 minutes. Drain and discard liquid. Stir in 1 tablespoon of oil and season with salt.

Add fish, cucumber, tomatoes, olives and basil to the beans and toss gently, making sure not to break up the fish pieces. Arrange the greens on a platter and add bean mixture.

Combine lemon juice in a bowl with a pinch of salt; whisk to dissolve salt. Whisking constantly, drizzle in remaining oil until mixture thickens slightly. Pour over salad and toss lightly.

Potato Stew with Red Onions, Tomatoes and Green Olives

Simplicity itself, this rustic stew from the Languedoc area of France is sensational served with a baked fish or any kind of roast meat or poultry. For this type of slow-cooking, the quality of your saucepan is of utmost importance. Invest in a few top-quality cast-iron, enamel-lined pans in different sizes. They will last a lifetime or longer.

MAKES 6 SIDE-DISH OR 4 LIGHT MAIN-COURSE SERVINGS

2 tablespoons extra-virgin olive oil

2 red onions, halved and cut into 3/4-inch (2-cm) slices

2 cloves garlic, chopped

2 lb. (1kg) waxy potatoes, peeled and cut into 3/4-inch slices

6 plum tomatoes, peeled, seeded and chopped

18 green olives, pitted, chopped

1/2 cup (120ml) water

Salt and black pepper

Combine oil and onions in a heavy Dutch oven and cook over medium heat until soft, stirring frequently, about 5 minutes. Add garlic and stir until aromatic, about 1 minute. Add potatoes, tomatoes, olives and water, and season to taste with salt and pepper. Bring to a simmer, cover and cook over low heat until the potatoes are tender, about 25 minutes. Stir gently from time to time, taking care not to break the potato slices. If during cooking the stew seems too dry, add a few tablespoons hot water. If there's a lot of liquid left in the pan, cook 5 to 10 minutes with the lid off to slightly thicken the sauce.

Potato Salad
with Olives, Capers and Herbs

You can never have enough potato salads in your repertoire, and here's a great addition. As with all good potato salads, probably the single most important thing is to toss the potatoes with the dressing while still warm, and to serve at room temperature. I particularly like this with cold, rare roast beef, such as Garlic Pot Roast (see page 86).

MAKES 4 TO 6 SIDE-DISH SERVINGS

2 oz. (60g) black olives, pitted and halved

1 tablespoon capers, drained and coarsely chopped

3 tablespoons chopped fresh oregano

10 large mint leaves, chopped

2 cloves garlic, chopped

1/4 cup (60ml) extra-virgin olive oil

1-1/2 lb. (750g) waxy potatoes

Salt and black pepper

Combine olives, capers, oregano, mint, garlic and oil in a large bowl; set aside.

Cook potatoes in boiling, salted water until tender, then drain. While still warm, cut into bite-sized pieces and immediately toss with the dressing. Let stand 20 minutes before serving at room temperature.

Cauliflower, Olive and Bell Pepper Salad

This salad is customarily served in Italy on Christmas Eve. Traditionally on this night, seven fish dishes are served. An eel dish, mussels, pasta with clam sauce, as well as this salad, which contains anchovies, are almost mandatory. The fish dishes have been attributed to the seven gifts from the Holy Spirit: wisdom, understanding, counsel, fortitude, knowledge, piety and fear of the Lord.

MAKES 4 TO 6 SIDE-DISH SERVINGS

2 red or yellow bell peppers, quartered lengthwise

1 cauliflower, divided in florets

1/4 cup (60ml) kalamata olives, pitted

4 anchovies, well rinsed and halved

1 tablespoon capers, rinsed and drained

2 tablespoons extra-virgin olive oil

1-1/2 tablespoons red wine vinegar

Salt and black pepper

Preheat the broiler. Broil the bell peppers, skin-side up, until blistered all over. Remove to a bowl, cover with plastic wrap and allow to sweat 20 minutes. When cool, rub off skin and remove membranes and seeds. Cut into thin strips and place in a salad bowl.

Bring a large saucepan of salted water to a boil, add cauliflower and, as soon as the water returns to a boil, drain cauliflower and rinse under cold water. When cool, add to the salad bowl.

Add olives, anchovies and capers; drizzle with oil and vinegar. Lightly season to taste with salt and pepper. Toss gently and serve at room temperature. If refrigerating, return to room temperature before serving.

Zucchini, Tomato and Olive Gratin with Thyme

Because zucchini has a rather bland flavor, it combines well with other, more assertive flavors, such as thyme. This gratin, with Provençal flavors, is terrific when served with roasted meat or a robust grilled fish.

MAKES 4 SIDE-DISH SERVINGS

4 teaspoons plus 1 tablespoon extra-virgin olive oil

1 onion, halved and thinly sliced

2 large cloves garlic, finely chopped

1 tablespoon fresh thyme leaves, chopped

2 tablespoons chopped parsley

Salt and black pepper

4 plum tomatoes, sliced

6 kalamata olives, pitted, chopped

1-1/4 lb. (635g) zucchini, sliced

1-3/4 cups (425ml) fresh breadcrumbs

Lemon wedges, to serve

Preheat oven to 375F (190C).

Combine 2 teaspoons of oil with onion in a frying pan and cook over medium heat until onion is soft, stirring frequently, about 5 minutes. Stir in garlic, and half the thyme and parsley. Season to taste with salt and pepper. Spread into a gratin dish and sprinkle with tomato slices and olives.

Heat another 2 teaspoons oil in the frying pan and add zucchini slices, remaining thyme and parsley.

Season lightly with salt and sauté until zucchini starts to lightly brown, stirring frequently, about 10 minutes. Spoon zucchini into the gratin dish, top with breadcrumbs and drizzle with the 1 tablespoon oil. Cover with foil and bake 15 minutes. Remove foil and bake 10 minutes more, or until the top is golden and crisp. Serve hot, warm or at room temperature, with lemon wedges.

Roasted Tomato
and Arugula Salad

Instead of goat cheese, this salad may be made successfully with bocconcini *(marinated fresh mozzarella) or a mild-flavored feta cheese. Serve as a starter to a summer meal or as a light lunch or supper dish.*

MAKES 4 FIRST-COURSE OR LIGHT
MAIN-COURSE SERVINGS

Marinade

1/2 cup (120ml) extra-virgin olive oil

Juice of half a lemon

1/4 cup (60ml) fresh basil leaves

1/4 cup (60ml) fresh parsley leaves

1 tablespoon fresh oregano leaves

2 cloves garlic, roughly chopped

8 oz. (60g) goat cheese, cut into
   4 thick slices

4 plum tomatoes, halved

Salt

1/4 cup (60ml) rosemary sprigs

1 bunch arugula

1 red onion, thinly sliced

To make the marinade: Combine all ingredients in a food processor or blender and process until smooth.

Place a single layer of cheese in a dish and pour over marinade. Cover with plastic wrap and refrigerate at least 2 hours, basting from time to time.

Meanwhile, preheat oven to 375F (190C). Arrange tomatoes in a baking dish, cut side up. Season lightly with salt and sprinkle with rosemary sprigs.

Bake 45 to 60 minutes, or until tomatoes start to become wrinkly and dried out. Allow to cool.

Thirty minutes before serving, remove cheese from refrigerator. Place arugula leaves on a platter and arrange tomatoes and onion on top. Add cheese and spoon the remaining marinade over the salad.

Index